# ECONOMIC DEVELOPMENT
# AND NATION BUILDING IN ETHIOPIA

# ECONOMIC DEVELOPMENT
# AND NATION BUILDING IN ETHIOPIA

## DANIEL TEFERRA

## FERRIS STATE COLLEGE

Distributed by:
Ferris State College
International Programs
Big Rapids, MI 49307

To my brother Yohannes (Johnny) who always assumed responsibilities in our family bigger than his age. His disappearance is like death yet has no ending.

And to my children Doyo and Samra.

"The traditional weakness, which is almost congenital to the national consciousness of underdeveloped countries, is not solely the result of the mutilation of the colonized people by the colonial regime. It is also the result of the intellectual laziness of the national middle class, of its spiritual penury, and the profoundly cosmopolitan mold that its mind is set in."

Frantz Fanon, <u>The Wretched of the Earth</u>

# Contents

# Preface

After neoclassical econo-mics abandoned the political economy approach of investigating society, economic development had been neglected until the post-Second World War period. The competition between the two super powers, the abject conditions, and the struggle for independence and progress in the Third World have triggered a new interest in economic development since the end of the War.

Mainstream theorists argued that the problem with the

Third World was the lack of capital, and saw that the transfer of capital from the center to the periphery was the only solution to the problem. They discounted the negative impacts of colonialism, and even considered it as a necessary stage in modernization. They believed that although colonialism was doubtless profitable, it was not exploitative—indeed it and it alone developed the base for industrial liftoff.

It is true that capital accumulation is essential for economic development, but the neoclassical analysis presents a fundamental flaw in ignoring historical and other non-economic dimensions of the development process.

Neo-Marxist-Leninist theorists, on the other hand, presented a counter-argument holding the center primarily accountable for the past and continuing problems of the Third World for exploiting economic surplus through colonialism and neocolonialism. Therefore, this analysis saw socialism and disengagement from the center as an essential and necessary requirement for progress and ending dependency in the Third World. This theory added a new insight into the process of economic development, but by emphasizing the impact of the center on the periphery, it failed to give sufficient attention to specific conditions in the Third World.

While one sees the center as the solution to the problem in the Third World, the other sees it as the main reason for the problem. Whether the center is the problem or the solution, external factor is secondary; not primary in economic development. Furthermore, a country develops not because it declares itself capitalist or socialist. Of course, an economic system is an important input to development, but for economic development to occur from within or by borrowing and domesticating modern technology, there has to be, first and foremost, an active nucleus of technical, professional and leadership resources from which further growth and stability are assured. The problems and prospects for the formation of this internal structure in Ethiopia are discussed from inter-disciplinary and historical perspectives.

This book addresses a new direction in economic development theory; and is the first to present a comprehensive study about economic development and popular unity in Ethiopia.

Big Rapids, Michigan                    Daniel Teferra
U.S.A.

# 1

# <u>Introduction</u>

Since the end of the Second World War, the question of economic development has become a dominant concern of contemporary social sciences. Economics, political science, history, sociology and psychology have converged upon a theory of economic development. But the interest in creating a theory of development is a recent phenomenon; and consequently an adequate theory in this area is not yet fully developed.

The relation between development theory and practice is like that of science and technology. There is no effective technology without adequate science or systematic knowledge. In the same way, there can be no effective development without adequate theoretical understanding.

The existing theories cannot adequately explain the problems of economic development and nation building in the Third World, in general, or in Ethiopia, in particular.

There are two major doctrines that attempt to explain the lack of development in the Third World: the mainstream school on one hand, and the neo-Marxist-Leninist on the other.

The mainstream doctrine attempts to explain the lack of development by comparing the conditions of the industrialized and non-industrialized countries, and then identifying a summary of economic, sociological and psychological features, considered typical of a traditional society.[1]

Furthermore, the mainstream school believes that external intrusion by industrialized capitalist countries into traditional societies is a necessary stage in modernization.[2] Consequently, the transfer of capital and modern technology from the West and the openness of trade with the capitalist world are viewed as essential elements for progress in the Third World.

In short, the mainstream school argues that the problem in the Third World is insufficient spread of capitalism. This theory identifies some of the critical problems facing the Third World countries.

However, it emphasizes disciplinary, mechanical aspects and ignores specific conditions of the Third World, as well as the negative impacts of external forces, particularly colonialism of the capitalist system on internal development. This theory presents a fundamental flaw in ignoring the historical dimension of economic development. Consequently, it cannot presume to attain a high degree of generality. By treating economic development essentially as the outcome of external forces, the mainstream school denies the Third World a history of its own.

It is rightly argued by mainstream development theorists that there is a positive correlation between economic development and nation building. National unity provides political stability that is essential for rapid economic growth. Furthermore, increasing national integration is equated with modernity.

A modern nation-state is seen as one that has a politics of nationalism within the context of state institutions. The politics of nationalism occurs after the gaps between elites and non-elites and between the modern and traditional sectors are closed by the performance of the middle level elites.[4]

Thus, because of the linkage between economic development and national integration, the process of nation building in the Third World has been a major concern among development theorists. Many theorists have stressed the political forms and conditions which may impede progress in the Third World.[5]

The implication here is that the new states in the Third World have not yet become nations. It is argued that the following factors are responsible for the absence of nationhood in the Third World: ethnic heterogeniety, social cleavages (rural-urban gaps, desparate levels of development within a territory, and gaps between elites and non-elites) and lack of shared political culture and legitimizing doctrine.[6]

It is true, particularly in Africa, that the lack of national integration has contributed to political instability, which in turn has made economic development a difficult process. But it is often assumed that the high degree of ethnic diversity is primarily responsible for the lack of national unity.[7]

**Ethnic diversity in Africa is not primarily responsible for the lack of national integration. Although internal divisions**

of African states attest to the importance of ethnic sentiment (the so-called tribalism), ethnic sentiment, despite its obvious influence, does not dominate African politics.[8]

The majority of the population in Africa rely more on kinship or ethnic groups for their material and security needs than on the state centers. The people, therefore, give their loyalty more to traditional sources of security and indentity. It is the failure of the state centers to replace these traditional    . sources that is mostly misunderstood as "tribalism" in Africa.

In addition, in the West, ethnic diversity did not prevent national integration. During the nineteenth century, the process of nation building took two forms. On the one side was the state-nation: nations formed by the state (England, France, the United States of America), in which the idea of national consciousness developed within the core of the state and a sense of nationhood transcended ethnic differences. On the other side was the nation-state: states formed from nations (Central and Eastern Europe), in which ethnic and political frontiers coincided and the idea of nationhood developed within the core of the individual culture.[9]

The second development doctrine, the neo-Marxist-Leninist school, radically departs from the mainstream notions treating the lack of development in the Third World essentially as the product of the same historical process that created the development of the capitalist world.[10]

According to the neo-Marxist-Leninist school, the problem in the Third World is imperialism of the capitalist system that created a class structure, blocking the development process in the periphery. The domination of Third World countries by an alliance between local elites and international capital assured that the economic surplus would not be used to promote capital accumulation in those areas; instead, the surplus would either be squandered unproductively by the local elites or directed abroad and used to further development in the already advanced capitalist countries.

At the center of all the neo-Marxist-Leninist analyses lies the recognition that capitalism is an international phenomenon in which the riches of the advanced capitalist countries and the problem in the Third World are tied together. Thus, capitalism is the problem rather than the solution to the Third World. Capitalism is not an option for the Third World whether or not it has benefited the now advanced countries. Socialism and disengagement from the captialist world are seen as an essential and indispensable condition for attaining economic development and ending dependency in the Third World.[11]

By considering the problem of economic development within a historical framework of the capitalist system, the neo-Marxist-Leninist school gives us a valuable insight into the process of development. However, it emphasizes capitalist expansion as the primary cause for lack of development in the Third World and fails to focus centrally on the productivity of labor as the essence and key to economic development.[12] Furthermore, its historical framework starts from the time capitalism emerged on the world scene rather than from the beginning of history. Thus, it ignores the impact of non-capitalist forces on internal development.

By prescribing socialism and disengagement from the capitalist world as a solution to the problem of the Third World, the neo-Marxist-Leninist analysis attempts to provide a political counter-argument to the position of the mainstream school.

Classical Marxism does not basically conceive of socialism in terms of economic development. Although the term "economic development" does not appear in classical Marxism, not only did Marxism state a general theory of society that was developmental in essence, it dealt with the problems of the emergence of modern society.

Thus, according to classical Marxism, economic development is essentially a process of capitalist enterprise. It is true that Marxism distinguishes lower and higher stages of communist society and envisages a full economic abundance only in the higher phase. However, the advance from the lower to the higher stage will not involve industrialization for the world that the workers were destined to win would already be highly industrialized and ripe for abundance.[13]

Regarding the question of nationhood, the neo-Marxist-Leninist school argues that the national-state expressed the aspiration of the rising middle class for economic unity and cultural freedom as against the restrictive elements of feudal society.[14]

However, according to this theory because of imperialism arising towards the end of the nineteenth century as a special stage in the development of capitalism, nationalism in the advanced countries ceased to serve the purpose of realizing internal unification, freedom, liberation and self-determination. Instead, nationalism became a weapon in the world struggle among rival capitalist groups for colonial occupation of the rest of the world. Furthermore, nationalism acquired its earlier functions and significance for the first time in the backward and colonial areas of the world in the period of imperialism.

Thus, the neo-Marxist-Leninist school treats the Third World countries as colonial countries, inhabited by colonial peoples, even though they may be formally independent nations. Third World countries are seen as the object of imperialist economic exploitation led by a small, colonial bourgeoisie, serving as an agent of imperialist rule.[15]

In addition, because of the contradiction of imperialism both in the industrialized nations and colonial countries, socialist opposition to imperialism will develop in the two worlds under the leadership of the working class. The two opposition forces are united in their immediate objectives and ultimate resolve to work for a socialist world system and full democracy.[16]

As the neo-Marxist-Leninist doctrine rightly points out, the expansion of the capitalist system in the late nineteenth century had a significant impact on the formations of the states in the Third World, particularly in Africa. However, the concept of nationalism is not a new phenomenon that emerged only in the late nineteenth century. Nationalism existed in the Third World, although in crude form, before imperialism of the capitalist system. Furthermore, the neo-Marxist-Leninist theory underestimates bourgeois democracy but does not adequately explain how full democracy can be reached under the so-called "working class dictatorship."

While both doctrines help our understanding of the development and nation building processes, they have problems of their own. Since there is no simple set of features that can explain economic development and nation building, an interdisciplinary perspective and the historical context of the development process are of basic importance. From every point of view, the advent of Western industrial democracy is a phenomenon whose understanding is of extraordinary importance for the purpose of analyzing the problems of economic development and nation building in Ethiopia.

The lack of economic development in Ethiopia revolves primarily around the low productivity of labor, which in turn is caused by the low level of technical skills and professionalism. On the other hand, the absence of the essential elements of popular unity has made it difficult to realize internal unification.

The following discussions will check, first, the existing theories against the Ethiopian experience; then bear out Ethiopia's problems of development and national unity; analyze the prospects for development and national integration; and finally present a conclusion.

# 2

# Theory and Reality

Mainstream Development Theory

The starting point in the mainstream economic development theory is "the vicious circle of poverty" thesis, advanced by Ragnar Nurkse. In his work, Problems of Capital Formation in Underdeveloped Countries, Nurkse states that a "circular constellation of forces," acting and reacting upon one another, keep a poor country in a continuous state of poverty. "A country is poor because it is poor,"[1] Nurkse says.

Attributing underdevelopment primarily to lack of capital formation, Nurkse spells out two circular relationships that hinder capital formation in poor countries. One limits the inducement to invest while the other limits the supply of saving.

As far as the inducement to invest is concerned, Nurkse argues that in poor countries, people's income is low and their purchasing power limited. In turn, this limits the size of the market thereby creating little or no incentive for entrepreneurs to invest. The small capital formation again limits worker productivity and keeps income low; thus perpetuating the circle.[2]

Regarding the supply of saving which Nurkse considers a more serious problem, the low income in poor countries limits the capacity to save thereby restricting the availability of funds for investment purposes. The small capital per worker again limits productivity and keeps income low; thus completing the circle.[3]

Nurkse identifies some of the critial problems of underdeveloped countries. But his argument, both on the demand and supply sides of investment, seems less weighty.

Writing in the tradition of the mainstream school, Assefa Bequele and Eshetu Chole in their collaborative work, A Profile of the Ethiopian Economy, ascribe the lack of development in Ethiopia to the narrowness of markets and low income of the population which reduced the incentives to sustain adequate investments in manufacturing.[4] But, neither the narrowness of markets nor low income is adequate to account for the problem of economic development in Ethiopia.

It is true that, relatively, markets have not been developed in Ethiopia. But, traditionally, there existed fairly extensive fairs and markets for foodstuffs, ivory, handicraft, livestock and livestock products, including luxury items for the ruling elites.[5]

Furthermore, although Ethiopia has remained a predominantly subsistence economy, a number of agricultural products such as coffee, livestock and livestock products, oilseeds, grains, pulses, cotton, etc., have enjoyed national and international markets since the Second World War.

In Ethiopia, there has been a market for products commonly consumed by the majority of the population. For example, in the 1960's, a successful expansion took place in such products as sugar, beverages, textiles, clothing, rubber sandals, canvas and leather footwears, various leather products, matches, soaps and food products.[6] In view of this, therefore, the lack of markets per se has not acted as a limit on investment.

A development process does not require that a low income country should have a large market to justify the production of every industrial product. What is needed is a market that is sufficient to absorb a range of products in order to get the process of economic growth under way.[7]

In low income countries, generally, domestic saving is not abundant; and consequently capital is lacking. However, this does not mean that everybody in a low income country is poor. There are elite groups that make fortune through various means. Even if capital is absolutely lacking, it can be borrowed from external sources.[8]

Richard Pankhurst, in his Economic History of Ethiopia, 1800-1935, rightly states that the limited innovating interests of most of the rulers and other conservative groups hindered economic development in Ethiopia.[9] Pankhurst, however, does not analyze his views in order to show how these groups inhibited economic development.

In Ethiopia, most of the imperial rulers and their associates were truly opposed to economic growth and technical innovation. They opposed Western ideas and innovations that threatened their interests. They amassed wealth through various means to pursue their own elite status rather than invest in production techniques.

Considering an intrusion by industrialized nations of the West as a necessary precondition for growth, Margery Perham states that Ethiopia's lack of development was the price paid for retaining independence. According to Perham, Ethiopia was denied, for the most part, the better production methods, the new cash crops, the transportation systems and the organized contacts with the world market, which were available to the colonial territories in Africa.[10]

But, Western colonialism did not actually provide better production methods to colonial Africa. Its primary objective was to turn Africa into a source of cheap labor and raw materials, and a market for export of surplus goods, labor and capital. By pursuing its own interest, Western capitalism, in fact, accomplished quite the opposite of improving the traditional production methods in Africa.[11] Hence, in terms of economic development, there is no significant distinction between Ethiopia and the colonial territories of Africa; consequently Ethiopia's lack of development cannot be treated as the price paid for retaining independence.

It is argued that the basic limiting factor of economic development in Ethiopia is the mountainous nature of the country, which makes the building of adequate network of motor roads difficult and very costly. Thus, it is believed that Ethiopia's agricultural surplus will remain locked in its mountains until the transportation system is highly developed. Furthermore, the enormous capital required for rapid growth, is not available internally, and investment funds from external sources are shrinking. Accordingly, it is difficult for Ethiopia to achieve economic progress.[12]

Infrastructure facilities play significant roles in the process of economic development. But a comprehensive infrastructure program cannot be treated as a prerequisite to economic growth. Any kind of infrastructure facility such as transportation, power, or communication can be built in various grades or sizes. Thus, there is no need for expensive infrastructures as such. The unit cost of a large infrastructure facility built so early will be very high since only a small fraction of the capacity will be used. Furthermore, big infrastructure facilities have their proper place in the course of economic development. Various development experiences suggest that economic growth has begun without massive investments in infrastructure facilities.[13]

Donald Levine, on the other hand, in his Wax and Gold: Tradition and Innovation in Ethiopian Culture, attributes Ethiopia's problem of national economic development primarily to what he calls the "individualism" and "orality syndrome" of the Amhara culture.

According to Levine, the Amhara ethnic group is highly individualistic and lacks the solidaristic traits that are common among the non-Amhara such as the Oromo or the Gurage in Ethiopia or other African groups. Hence, according to Levine, the individualistic traits and the consequent atomism of the Amhara have not been conducive to mobilize the energies and to provide the organization and the creative leadership required for Ethiopia's modernization.[12]

Levine makes incisive observations about the sociopsychological factors of the traditional Amhara culture. The impact of the Amhara culture on Ethiopia and its development process cannot be underestimated.

However, development is mainly an economic process although it has social, political and other dimensions. Economic development is not a function of certain psychological characteristics. If it is believed that economic development is determined by certain psychological factors, the logical conclusion will be that people in the industrialized countries have superior traits while those in the low income countries have inferior traits. Similarly, within a low income country itself, it will imply that certain ethnic groups cannot develop because they lack the psychological traits essential for economic development. A psychological theory of development is incorrect since it makes distinction among peoples on the basis of racial or ethnic traits.

Furthermore, the aspects of individualism and orality syndrome, stated by Levine as peculiar to the Amhara, are by no means limited to the Amhara culture. They exist in other cultures of the industrialized and low income countries. The non-Amhara groups in Ethiopia or in the rest of Africa, which are believed by Levine to have solidaristic traits, did not actually forge ahead in the development race. It was, in fact, the Amhara who introduced to the non-Amhara groups agricultural innovations, centralized administration and literature, something which Western colonialism had failed to accomplish in Africa.

## Neo-Marxist-Leninist Theory

Much of the foundation for the neo-Marxist-Leninist theory was laid by Paul Baran. The theory regards underdevelopment essentially as the product of the same historical process which resulted in the development of the advanced capitalist countries. In other words, development and underdevelopment are treated as the opposite sides of the same coin.

The mainstream theory of development, for example, treats the infusion of capital and new technology resulting from trade and other forms of contact with the advanced capitalist countries as a powerful stimulus to development.

On the contrary, the neo-Marxist-Leninist theory argues that although contact with Western technology provides a powerful impetus to development, this development is "forcibly shunted off its normal course, distorted and crippled to suit the purposes of Western imperialism."[15] This is due to the transfer of surplus and resources from the underdeveloped to the developed countries, and continued technological, financial and cultural dependency of the former on the latter.

By regarding underdevelopment essentially as the product of the same historical process which generated the capitalist world, the neo-Marxist-Leninist theory rejects the notion that underdevelopment is a peculiar or an inherent characteristic of underdeveloped countries thereby breaking with the mainstream school.

Baran's basic thesis received considerable elaboration from Andre Gunder Frank, Paul Sweezy, and Samir Amin. Drawing on Baran's argument, Andre Gunder Frank concludes that "underdevelopment is not due to the survival of archaic institutions and the existence of capital shortage in regions that have remained isolated from the stream of world history. On the contrary, underdevelopment was and still is generated by the very same historical process which also generated economic development: the development of capitalism itself."[16]

Writing in the same tradition, Samir Amin, in his Unequal Development, states that the phenomenon of underdevelopment had begun to appear in Ethiopia after the Italian conquest of 1935, particularly after the Second World War when Ethiopia was completely integrated into the capitalist world system.[17]

We may ask, then, to what extent can the phenomenon of underdevelopment in Ethiopia be understood as a direct product of the past and continuing development of the capitalist world?

Western penetration in general, and Italian expansion in particular, were indeed inimical to Ethiopia's development and unity in the last quarter of the nineteenth century. At this time, Western powers were engaged in forceful commercial and military intrusions into northeast Africa to which the creation of the Italian colony of Eritrea, against the interest of Ethiopia, bore testimony.[18]

In addition, the Italians occupied Ethiopia proper in 1936. Although the occupation lasted only five years, the Italian colonialism had impacted the development of Ethiopia. This was more visible on Ethiopia's external trade.

Ethiopia's external trade was restructured to fit the Italian economy. Imports increased substantially while exports declined even below the lowest levels of the pre-colonial period. As a result, Ethiopia registered deficit trade balances for the first time in history. In addition, the disruption in trade and incentives caused the market for food staples to decline.[19]

Relative to trade, the colonial impact on the traditional agriculture was small. Expropriation of land took place, but not on a large scale as in the case of colonial Africa. On the other hand, significant wage and compulsory-labor demands were imposed on the peasant population. The Italians also appropriated Ethiopia's gold reserves and production.[20]

On the positive side of the balance sheet, Italian colonialism enhanced the wage system against the widespread corvée and slave labor of the traditional economy. The Italians spent an amount considered the highest in colonial Africa on infrastructure development. They built new all-weather roads with tunnels, bridges and escarpment buttresses applying their innovative and engineering skills. Hospitals, schools, and municipal buildings were constructed although they were all for the Italians. Investments were made in various commercial enterprises and consumer goods industries.[21]

Although it cannot be denied that some benefits trickled down to the population, the colonial system as a whole was founded upon the neglect and exploitation of the majority of the Ethiopians.[22]

Thus, it can be concluded safely that the Italian colonialism acted as an impedement to the economic development of Ethiopia. However, it was not primarily responsible for the lack of development in Ethiopia. Ethiopia's development had been already unpromising before the Italians came.[23] Therefore, it cannot be argued that the coming of the Italian colonialism choked off a promising development in Ethiopia to the extent of causing its failure to modernize.

Ethiopia's contact with the capitalist world has increased since the Second World War. However, it is questionable whether such contact can be assigned primary responsibility for the lack of development in Ethiopia.

In the first place, the flow of direct foreign investment into Ethiopia since the end of the War has not been significant. Secondly, foreign investment rather stimulated the formation of domestic capital.[24] Furthermore, direct foreign investment did not merely go for extractive enterprises to feed Western centers. Foreign investment, in cooperation with domestic capital, was used for the establishment of enterprises that produced commodities for internal consumption and exports. It provided employment opportunities to Ethiopians. Similarly, government borrowing from the outside world played a significant role in financing economic projects and infrastructure.

During the post-War period (1960-1974), more capital came into Ethiopia than left (refer to Appendix I). Foreign corporations in Ethiopia financed their expansion mainly with new captial inflow rather than with retained earnings (refer to Appendix II). Generally, repatriation of profits, dividends and capital was not large enough to the extent of offsetting new capital inflow. Repayments on government borrowing did not exceed proceeds from new loans although annual payments were on the rise (refer to Apendix I).

It needs to be mentioned that besides the effects on balance of payments, direct foreign investment benefits a country economically if it yields a net increase in value added—a net increase in the incomes of domestic workers, domestic supplies, and customer and other firms affected by the operation.[25]

There is no evidence to support the argument that the post-War contact with the West was harmful to Ethiopia, and consequently be assigned the primary responsibility for Ethiopia's failure to modernize and end dependency.

In the post-1974 period, foreign capital has played a significant role in Ethiopia's development programs. Ethiopia still relies in large part on the West for both trade and development assistance compared to its new allies in the Eastern bloc.[26]

By assuming that direct relations with the capitalist world creates unfavorable consequences to the Third World, the neo-Marxist-Leninist theory implies that breaking out of such relations will create favorable consequences. But this is not always true.

In fact, in light of the growing efforts by socialist countries to attract Western technology and finance,[27] the argument that the Third World will achieve economic development and end dependency through socialism and disengagement from the capitalist world becomes less weighty. Furthermore, as a result of changes in internal factors and the operation of imperialism of the capitalist system, economic growth and industrialization have occured as rapidly and consistently in certain areas of the periphery.[28]

However, the problems that the Third World faces in its relations with the industrialized capitalist countries cannot be ignored. Much of the foreign investment in Third World is undertaken by multinational corporations which have become major actors in the world's political economy.

The record of multinational corporations regarding their role in international development is a mixed bag. The major goal of the multinational corporations is to maximize world-wide profits which does not always coincide with development interests of host countries. In some places, multinational corporations have played significant roles in bringing capital and technology to the Third World. But some of the activities of multinational corporations, although pursued in the best interest of business, have conflicted with the development objectives and national interests of host countries.

Some multinational corporations are criticized for practicing tax evasion; for manipulating financial flows through the use of artificial or transfer prices; limiting exports of their affiliates; allocating markets and restricting the use of their technology through intra-firm trade; and finally, for carrying out unethical activities.[29]

The neo-Marxist-Leninist theory rightly directs our attention to the historical process of development. But its historical process is not complete for it discusses the advent and expansion of capitalism only. As a result, it ignores noncapitalist expansions such as Islamic commerce and ideology that had impacted the Ethiopian development.[30]

Regarding the question of national unity, the neo-Marxist-Leninist approach does not provide us with a convincing argument. For example, Addis Hiwet and Bereket Habte

Selassie argue that the Ethiopian nation was created in the late nineteenth century by the Shawa-Amhara colonial conquest in cooperation with imperialism of the capitalist system. Thus, the self-determination of the conquered nations under the leadership of the working class is treated as the prerequisite to national integration and complete democracy in Ethiopia.[31]

Both writers ignore and caricature facts. The national foundation of Ethiopia was rooted in the Axumite Empire (in present-day Tigrai). The Amhara emerged at the beginning of the second millenium A.D., and have since been the main political heirs of the Axumites. They inherited from Axum, a plow-based mixed agriculture, the Orthodox Christian Church, and the imperial system of rule.[32]

Between the thirteenth and sixteenth centuries, the Shawa-Amhara instituted the gult (fief) economy, a secular administration, a common language, literature and arts to express the aspiration of Ethiopian nationalism, and used Semetic elements such as the Solomonic Dynasty and the Axumite Christianity to unite the Ethiopian empire.[33] The late nineteenth century, therefore, cannot be taken as the starting point of Ethiopia*. It is true, of course, that the reconstruction of Ethiopia as a centralized, modern political state, from a loose federation of kingdoms within a dynastic empire, began in the last quarter of the nineteenth century.[34]

The principle of self-determination does not fit the people of Ethiopia. There have been close, historical and geographic connections among the people of northern Ethiopia although the same parallel may not be drawn between the north and the south for serious contact with the south began only in the

*Refer to Appendix III for a historical account of the Ethiopian social formation.

last quarter of the nineteenth century. However, the contact with the south did not produce a colonial relationship similar to that found in overseas empires of Western powers.

The people of northern and southern Ethiopia were not strangers to each other as the British and the Kenyans were. There had been for centuries a continuous process of political, economic and cultural interactions among them.[35] There were never those feelings of biological or social superiority and inferiority which existed in the European colonial empires. A Shawa-Amhara settler held no special status or prestige due to his ethnic background. The natives did not show any special distaste for the Amhara culture. There was social intercourse between the two groups. The Shawa-Amhara intermarried with most groups they came in contact with despite some prejudice. It was mainly in matters of religion, language and culture that they considered themselves superior to the conquered people although they had little or no knowledge about the latter.

The self-determination principle is a simplistic answer to the problem of unity in Ethiopia. Even the Bolsheviks, the staunchest supporters of the self-determination thesis, were unable to implement it successfully as the economic and security considerations of the Russian state outweighed all other considerations.

Thus the Bolsheviks, including Lenin, were forced to perpetuate the Tsarist empire by adjusting mainly economic inequalities.[36] Only Finland and Poland succeeded in breaking away from the old Russian Empire due to special circumstances. In Finland, the victory of the anti-Soviet forces backed by the Germans led to the establishment of a sovereign state. The independence of Poland, on the other hand, was strongly advocated by the Bolsheviks and even by the Provisional Government for the Polish inhabited areas had already been occupied by the Germans and the Austrians.[37]

The significant difference in the history of the Russian and Ethiopian nationalities needs to be mentioned. Some of the Ethiopia's nationalities were incorporated into the Empire in the last quarter of the nineteenth century while they were still at a very low stage of development. Since then their situation has not changed significantly. They had had no experience of statehood before the integration; thus breaking up Ethiopia into separate ethnic nations will extremely imperil the security and economy of the State.

The Eritrean question, on the other hand, is a different matter. By the end of the last century, Eritrea was separated from the old Ethiopian Empire by the Italians and had since experienced a colonial statehood. In the course of fifty years of colonization, Eritrea generated a social class made up of civil servants; people employed in various branches of the economy, especially commerce and other professional services; and a few urban and rural landowners. This social class provided the political leadership that brought about the federation of Eritrea with Ethiopia in 1952, and consequently earned the Eritrean people the right to conduct their own affairs.

The Eritrean conflict was triggered by the continued interference of the "federal" government of Ethiopia in the internal affairs of Eritrea. In the end, Eritrea was brought under the direct control of the central government. This action intensified the conflict and renewed the old problem of regionalism.[38]

On top of the question of nationalities, we have to examine

carefully whether the working class ideology of Marxism-Leninism can be an effective force of national integration in Ethiopia.

Organized labor came into existence in Ethiopia just in the 1960's. Given the low level of industrialization, the labor movement has not yet made its presence felt in the political process of Ethiopia. Labor is a small minority in the Ethiopian population. The structure and consciousness of the working class in Ethiopia, or in Africa for that matter, are inadequate to provide a mass base for national unity for the following reasons.[39]

In the first place, the process of modernization in the West was a relatively rapid transition from a small to a large scale industrial production, accompanied by an emergence of a majority of wage-earning labor force in the population. In contrast, in Africa the process of industrialization generally took a different pattern and has been a slow process. Consequently, it has produced a slowly growing minority of wage-earning labor force in the population.

Secondly, since the process of urbanization has taken place without an all-round industrialization, the wage force in Africa is a minority of the urban population. In addition, workers in Africa have not yet formed a homogeneous group since they are still divided by ethnic, religious and other cleavages.

Although there is a relationship between workers and the rest of the population in Africa, the interest of the workers is not necessarily the same as that of the rest of the population. The relation in production and the protection and improvement needs of the workers are quite different .

The trade union movement in Africa was not built from below as such. The process in the nineteenth century England, for example, was from the guild and benefit society to the craft union and cooperative, and eventually to the national trade union movement and a mass worker-based labor party. In Africa, on the other hand, most trade union movements have been organized from above by nationalist politicians or corporatist states seeking effective control over the workers. In addition, in Africa workers lack leadership and consequently rely on non-worker professionals.

Workers in Africa do not have a higher level of political awareness than the rest of the population as such. They still exhibit ties of kinship to extended, patriarchal family and to ethnic groups; they show feelings of mini-nationalism, adherence to a particular religion or to a sect within a religion, and fatalistic attitudes.

The economic and social conditions necessary for the process of national integration along working class ideology are not present in Ethiopia or in Africa as a whole. Even if the conditions are present, there is no magic in class interest which will secure to members of one class the support of members of other classes. The success of any class in a national integration process depends on its ability to win support from outside its own membership which again will depend upon its fulfillment of tasks set by interests wider than its own.[40]

# 3

# Problems of Development and Nation Building

The lack of economic development in Ethiopia is attributable primarily to the low level of labor productivity which in turn is caused by the low level of technical skills and professionalism. On the other hand, the problem of national unity can be sought in the absence of the essential elements of a democratic political process.

Because there is no simple set of features that can explain the problems of economic development and nation building, it is of basic importance to examine the development process from interdisciplinary and historical perspectives.

The transformation of the West into a predominantly industrial economy took roughly three centuries of modern history. A number of social and economic factors that had been in the making for centuries ultimately formed the indispensable preparation for the final outburst of technological breakthrough in England first and then in the rest of the industrialized world. Thus, the problems facing Ethiopia and the rest of Africa can be analyzed in light of the socio-economic and political factors that led to economic development and popular unity in the West. [1]

## Agricultural Transformation

One of the factors essential for economic development is a successful and thorough transformation of subsistence agriculture into commercial farming. This process requires the introduction of major technical and biological advances in agriculture by departing from the traditional farming practices and land use patterns, and allowing enterprising farmers more scope and opportunities for permanent farming and independent experiments.

It requires landowners and farmers to find their profits in commerce and show interest in scientific agricultural improvements.

Agriculture has been the major economic base of Ethiopia for centuries. Grain cultivation began in Ethiopia thousands of years ago. The plow is at the center of traditional agriculture technique in Ethiopia.

Ethiopia's agricultural implements and practices have remained virtually unchanged for centuries. The plow and draught animals are not wide-spread. Farming is mainly carried out by hand with the help of machete, hoe and burning. The latter is also used to fertilize the soil despite the abundance of manure. While plowing, stones are left on the field to store up humidity and prevent erosion. Tree growing is not widely known as a land management practice. There are areas where crop farming is not yet known, and the sources of food supply are hunting, gathering and fishing.

Livestock rearing is at a relatively early stage, depending entirely on migratory pastoralism. This activity is usually carried out by separate ethnic groups who still live in semi-permanent homes and are not yet prepared to function at other than herding. The stubborn practice of migratory pastoralism and communal ownership of range lands and herds stand against the market concept and sedentary stock breeding.

One of the major impediments of agricultural improvement in Ethiopia was the land tenure system on which the imperial rule had rested for centuries. Traditionally, the livelihood of Ethiopian peasants depended on rist (in Amhara) and risti (in Tigrai) system that conferred heritable and inalienable rights to hold and farm ancestral land.[2] On the other hand, the imperial elites imposed gult (fief) system on rist to maintain themselves and their officials by drawing off the agricultureal surplus and labor of the peasants in the form of tributes.

Gult rights were taxing, judicial and administrative rights over the peasant holders, ristagnas, given to the imperial rulers, ecclesiastics, and members of the civilian and military administration, gultagnas, as payment for their services. Thus, almost all arable and inhabited land was granted out as gult. Although ristagnas were not considered tenants, their hereditary rist right depended on their meeting tax and service obligations to the gultagnas. In the south, however, where the gult system was pushed to its worst form, obligations of the peasants were onerous, and it was not always possible for peasants to move away to other estates.

Generally, the gultagnas were divorced from productive activities. They lived off the peasants and the surplus collected was mainly used for the maintenance of prestige, power and ligitimacy rather than for agricultural improvement.

The process of bureaucratic modernization finally abolished the gult system by 1966. The establishment of a modern army reduced the military significance of the gultagnas. A new system of taxation was instituted that abolished payment in kind and services, and made taxes payable directly to the finance ministry. Tribute and tax, formerly received by government officials, were replaced by cash salary from the central government. Gult-holding religious establishments lost most of their secular authority over their peasants but still controlled extensive lands and received a portion of the land tax.

The bureaucratic reform did not radically alter the status of the traditional rentier groups. The former gultagnas were immediately made government officials and compensated with grants of land. The privilege system of rewarding loyal servants of the imperial system with land remained intact. All this generated complicated tenancy arrangements throughout the country to impede agricultural improvement.

The various landowning groups of the imperial family, nobles, officials and bureaucrats including soldiers and clerics lived off the ordinary peasants while they were actually divorced from and failed to improve agriculture on which their livelihood depended. Worse still, the traditional elites and their associates controlled the post-War government and the parliament from where they blocked the passage of land reform bills and modernizing programs.

The majority of the rural population lived as sharecroppers with income barely sufficient to provide for a narrowly defined subsistence minimum. Exorbitant rents and landlessness took away the incentive from the rural majority to improve agriculture.[3]

Besides the land tenure system, the conservative attitude and fatalism of the peasants have played a part in retarding agricultural development in Ethiopia. The Ethiopian peasants are not reform minded. However, they are generally found to be hardworking.

The Ethiopian peasants see working their land and living by the sweat of their brow as their main goal in life. They idealize agricultural work as a means of promoting the virtues of independence and honesty. There is little belief in the power of human beings over nature which is commonly accepted as more powerful than humans and something to be adjusted to rather than overcome and changed. Values and religious attitudes adhere to the belief that humans have no causal effect upon their own future: "God, not humans, can improve humans' lot." As a consequence, an attitude of resignation rather than innovation is fostered.[4]

The Ethiopian peasants are not, of course, totally opposed to change. They are receptive to change by following the directives and imitating the examples of their local authorities and as long as the change gives them immediate benefit and is in congruent with their beliefs and values.[5]

For example, in the north rist area, the attitude towards land reform was negative because it was often mistaken for the qelad system, land alienation and the abolition of the rist system. Small ristagnas favored the idea of equal distribution of land among households while big ristagnas strongly opposed such reform. Although land measurement was opposed as a prelude to the qelad system, ristagnas generally favored the idea of having their rist-lands registered in their own names in the government tax books for they felt this would help them defend their lands against the claims of others. In the south where sharecroppers and landless peasants were widespread, the idea of land reform was always welcome. It was seen as the restoration of the "independent" landholder system.[6]

Ethiopia has spent a relatively long time practicing subsistence agriculture, consisting mainly of undeveloped implements and farming skills. In the countryside, economic life, accidents of war and nature aside, has been unchanged from year to year. Economic development is a recent phenomenon. The introduction of agricultural innovations started in the 1960's in selected areas along the main roads by government bureaucracies. Commercial farming and plantation agriculture were initiated in very limited areas by small groups of enterprising individuals and foreign enterprises.[7]

Land reform, something new in the history of Ethiopia, came in 1975 under the Military Government. The reform program abolished landlord-tenant relationships and private property in land. Each farm family was allowed inheritable use rights of ten hectares of land.[8]

Land redistribution has only been carried out in some areas - mostly in the south and west. In the northwest where the rist system is deeply entrenched, land redistribution was met with opposition.

The military Government has organized agricultural production on the basis of associations, cooperatives and state

farms. But the results have not been promising due to inefficient management and lack of enthusiasm of the peasants to
work collectively. Yet, the Government has decided to speed
up the cooperativization program.[9] Bureaucratic control over
agricultural improvement has been strengthened leaving little or no room for local participation and independent practice by enterprising farmers.

The land reform, the literacy campaign, and the significant
increase in schools and health facilities are the real changes
brought about by the Military Government. Beyond this first
great step, material improvement in everyday living has not
yet come about. Ethiopia is still underdeveloped with widespread poverty.[10]

## Advancement in Commerce and Entrepreneurship

Another contributing factor to technical innovation and
economic growth is the advancement in commerce and entrepreneurship. One of the factors that distinguished England from other European nations in the eighteenth century
was that England had accumulated large amounts of capital.

A century of successful exploration, slave trading, piracy
war and commerce had made England the richest nation in
the world. It became the first nation to develop a mass consumer market; a prime requisite of an industrial economy.
The riches that accrued to the nobles and the large upper-
middle class created a rising pressure of demand inspiring a
search for new production techniques. Internal markets expanded and production techniques improved as the fusion
between commercial talents and technical skills gave rise to
an entirely new class of economically important persons:
industrial entrepreneurs.

Ethiopia, on the other hand, has not been a trading economy. After the Axumite Empire lost control of the trade route of the African Red Sea coast as early as the eighth century A.D., Ethiopia remained an isolated agricultural country for a long time, lying far beyond the horizon of Europe. Until the second half of the twentieth century, economic ties with the outside world were maintained through the surrounding Muslim establishments that minimized outside influences whenever they were in bad terms with Christian Ethiopia.[11]

In Ethiopia, the Christian community of nobles, priests, soldiers and cultivators had for centuries despised commerce and crafts. To a large extent trade passed into the hands of Muslims, who were excluded from government and land ownership until Haile Selassie's reign. The occupational separation between Christian and Muslim communities had been reinforced by the neighboring Muslim countries who preferred to deal with and favored Muslim merchants. Even in highland Ethiopia, the Christian merchant was always at a disadvantage when competing with the Muslim.[12]

Although the imperial elites despised the practice of commerce, they derived wealth from royal trade conducted through agents, tolls, custom duty, and market dues. They held a monopoly over the trade of lucrative products such as salt, ivory, and gold. During Haile Selassie's Regime, foundations and prize trusts were used to manage royal businesses.

Traditionally, the key merchants and artisans were always foreigners: Jews, Greeks, Armenians, Arabs, and Italians who made fortunes and lived under excellent conditions. But they were insecure as they often worked under pressure from the ruling elites. They shared their profits with the ruling elites as bribes and gifts, and pursued short term aims by investing their profits mostly abroad rather than in the country. Their contributions to commercial and technical improvements of the country were limited.

The expansion of economic activity in the post-War period helped the emergence of native merchants. But most of the native merchants were still engaged in simple mercantile activities as distributors of imports or buyers for foreign exporters. Those who were able to make fortune from their activities did not enjoy social status commensurate with their wealth. The imperial elites used various means to undermine the growth and influence of the merchant class.

For example, fines were imposed arbitrarily on merchants, and their property confiscated, or they were forced to donate money for so-called "charitable" causes. When private entrepreneurs became too successful, they were forced into government service. Licences were revoked or given to foreigners rather than to Ethiopians. Dividends from commercial enterprises were withheld or given to those favored by the Emperor. Fearing all this, Ethiopian entrepreneurs used foreigners to run their businesses.[13]

Investment in modern industries was a state monopoly through which the imperial elites pursued their own interests. The growth of potential entrepreneurs was discouraged. With the coming of the Military Government, leading merchants and potential entrepreneurs were squeezed out as public enterprises assumed most of the activities of the private sector.

## Work Ethic, Equality of Status and Social Mobility

The existence of a social system flexible enough to permit the rise of productive groups was one of the major factors responsible for technological breakthrough in the West. The flexibility of the social system made it possible to unleash and harness the energies of talented people in lower and middle ranks of the social order. In place of the old ideal of social and economic stability of knowing and keeping ones "social position", a new conception of economic life brought respectability to an ideal of hard work, saving, material improvement, and economic growth. The new social value approved of diligence, achievement through independent action, encouraged profit and wealth seeking, and provided the temper of a businesslike world. Wealth was to be accumulated and put to good use; not squandered.

In Ethiopia work as such is not deemed an absolute value. Productive work is discouraged by the common belief that "from working by hand comes servitude, from cleverness of mouth comes mastery." Working in the bureaucracy is considered a dignified work. Contact with the physical process of production is seen as soiling oneself with dirty work; thus it is considered undignified. Artisans, with the exception of the goldsmith, are despised and associated with the "evil eye." Menial labor is avoided because it is considered the work of slaves and "inferior" groups. Selling labor service for wages and mercantile spirit are looked down upon and relegated to "inferior" groups. Productive groups, with the exception of cultivators, have suffered social oppression and denied upward mobility.

The society does not consider the process of saving and investment as a virtue. The squandering of income is a common phenomenon among elites as well as ordinary people. It was not unusual for the imperial elites to legitimize their power and influence by squandering their wealth on palaces, churches, monasteries, lavish endowments, entertainments, and European furnishings.[15] The ordinary people emulated their leaders through various mechanisms of wasteful consumption despite meager incomes.

In Ethiopia status is ascribed rather than achieved by ones own hard work. The value system minimizes the importance of material rewards, independence, and economic calculation.

Traditionally, the society was hierarchically structured and upward mobility was limited. The royal nobility was a closed hereditary estate. There was some upward mobility to the non-royal nobility for Ethiopians of "low" birth as a result of showing exceptional ability in military and political affairs. However, even if a commoner was carried high in the political hierarchy by ability and fortune, he was not automatically accepted into the nobility for the Ethiopian nobility was already a self-conscious status group with hereditary base.

The main route to upward mobility was through the accumulation of land by pressing claims over others. This required skill and ability to litigate successfully. Those who had the ability to litigate successfully were usually the powerful and wealthy individuals who could buy witnesses and the courts to their side.[16]

Soldiering held out hopes of quick advancement through requisitioning, collecting booty and slave raiding. It offered opportunities of association with the imperial rulers and officials, security and rewards. Soldiering was seen by the peasantry as a better alternative to the drudgery of working in the field. Since the establishment of a modern army in the 1940's, military opportunities have increased, and the life and status of the Ethiopian soldiery have improved significantly.

Another avenue to upward mobility in Ethiopia was priesthood. Priests were accorded high respect and status in Christian Ethiopia, and had a significant social and political influence on the society. Generally, priests were poor. They acquired status and respect not from wealth but as a result of being teachers and preachers of the state religion. Attracted by the high status of priesthood and attachment of land, priests often trained their sons and relatives to succeed them, and they married into families of the same profession thereby making priesthood almost a hereditary caste.

The debtara (the scholar literati) were better off and more influential than the rest of the clerics. Trained in advanced theology for a number of years, the debtara served the Church as scholars, teachers, singers, and poets. They were scribes for the illiterate and pursued secular activities in the Church and government bureaucracies in different capacities. The debtara were known for their shrewdness and reputed traditional knowledge. Some of them turned their knowledge into a means of acquiring income by working as astrologers, fortune tellers, herbalists, and wizards.

The coming of modern education in the post-War period ended the monopoly of education enjoyed by the debtara, and created more and better opportunities for the modern intelligentsia who were able to possess various qualifications affording them a much better life and a feeling of superiority amidst a mass of illiterates.

The modern intelligentsia relied on the bureaucracy as the avenue to upward mobility. Very few exercised their individual initiatives and enterprising talents.

## A Spirit of Scientific Inquiry

The other main feature associated with technological advance and economic growth is a spirit of scientific inquiry. This leads to inventiveness and innovation. During the period of capitalist development in the West this was very much the case.

In Western Europe, starting in the late fourteenth century, the medieval view of the universe became transformed into scientific understanding of nature. Both the Renaissance and Reformation encouraged a sense of confidence in human ability to arrive at new truths about the physical environment. By the late seventeenth century, scientific knowledge was actively encouraged as a key to increasing human control over the environment. The scientific revolution contributed to the making of the modern world by providing a new conception and explaining the laws of nature.

The post-Renaissance intellectuals of Europe experienced a great surge of interest in scientific inquiry. Eighteenth century England became the focus of a unique enthusiasm of science and engineering. The famous Royal Society was founded in 1660 and became the immediate source of much intellectual excitement. A popular interest in technical devices of all sorts developed and the people identified with technological progress.

In Ethiopia, scientific inquiry has not completely replaced traditional thought patterns. Learning was highly valued by both Christians and Muslims but produced a class of literati for the purpose of transmitting religious beliefs and perpetuating old thinking and status quo. The traditional scholars possess a good understanding of their country and people although their outlook and knowledge about the outside world are limited.

The pursuit of new ideas has been discouraged by the religious belief that considers experimentation as a direct

challenge to the mysteries of God. Due to centuries of isolation from the rest of the world, the Ethiopian Church has
grown into a bastion of rigidity, defensiveness and conservative attitudes. It is interested in the Great Unknown of the
other world emphasizing the "higher good" rather than economic good. The clerics have been the leading opponents of
Western ideas and innovation.

Modern education is a recent phenomenon in Ethiopia. It
did not begin to spread until the 1940's. The coming of Western education initiated scientific inquiry and learning for the
sake of personal development.

The modern intelligentsia is small, young, and disunited.
Several factors account for this. In the first place, institutional facilities are inadequate, and academic freedom is unknown. There are few, if any, channels of communication for
Ethiopian intellectuals to develop their minds and stimulate
their imaginations. There is little contact with the outside
world, and Western-educated Ethiopians tend to end intellectual functions once they return home. They have not been a
significant and sophisticated social force to make their presence felt in the political process and economic development
of Ethiopia. Most of the intellectuals come from urban centers
and were conditioned by the "welfare school" system of free
room and board and tuition.[17] Their understanding of the
Ethiopian reality is limited.

Political orientation among the modern intelligentsia has
increased since the 1960 attempted coup d'etat, and intensified after the overthrow of Haile Selassie's Regime in 1975.
Marxism-Leninism was accepted for the first time as an offi-
cial doctrine and considerable time and energy have been
devoted to studying the ideology. However, no serious inves-
tigation has been made about its applicability to Ethiopia's

problems. This is not without consequences as the following summary from Amilcar Cabral,[18] which deserves to be quoted at some length, indicates:

"We must deeply analyze each situation to avoid loss of time and energy doing things that we are not to do and forgetting things that we have to do. . . . We base our struggle on the concrete realities of our country. We appreciate the experiences and achievements of other peoples and study them. But revolution or national liberation struggle is like a dress which must be fit to each individual's body. Naturally, there are certain general or universal laws; even scientific laws for any condition, but the struggle has to be developed according to the specific conditions of each country. This is fundamental. . . . The guerrilla manuals once told us that without mountains you cannot make guerrilla war. But in my country, there are no mountains, only the people. In the economic field, we committed an error. We began training our people to commit sabotage on the railroads. When they returned from their training, we remembered that there were no railroads in our country. . . . There are other conditions to consider as well. You must consider the type of society in which you are fighting- . . . . Some people tell us that our struggle is the same as that of the Vietnamese people. It is similar but not the same. The Vietnamese are a people that hundreds of years ago fought against foreign invaders like a nation. We are now forging our nation in the struggle. This is a big difference. . . . Vietnam is also a society with clear social structures with classes well defined. There is no national bourgeoisie in our country. A miserable petit bourgeoisie yes, but not a national bourgeoisie."

## Borrowing and Adapting Technology

Economic development can occur by borrowing and internalizing modern technology. This requires a progressive economy with a social class or group that can see profit in borrowing and adapting the modern technology.

During the second half of the nineteenth century, new machines, production methods, and ideas were introduced to

Europe from Britain. The spread of technical knowledge from Britain and the role played by British capital, entrepreneurs, managers and skilled labor in promoting economic development on the continent was significant. British capital and influence showed also great achievements in North America, Australia, New Zealand, South Africa and Argentina. British influence in such places as Sweden and Japan was small. Thus the development process there was mostly self-generated.[19]

Economic development proceeded fairly rapidly in the above countries and in some of them soon surpassed that of England. Progress had been underway in these countries before the coming of British influence, and they had acquired internal capabilities to borrow and domesticate modern technology.

The entire human history is filled with records of cultural and technological learning by one people from another. No people have a monopoly over the ability to develop science and technology. Yet, borrowing and adapting technology has not been an easy and simple process.

The Industrial Revolution that began in England by no means guaranteed the immediate establishment of the factory system in the rest of the world. In fact, the British sought to prevent the dissemination abroad of the details of the new inventions because new technology is a commercial product with a proprietory interest.

This British effort possibly accounted for a time lag of some years in the introduction of the new machines to the United States and other places. On the other hand, the new techniques could be imported since American entrepreneurs with sufficient capital became aware of the possibilities of employing them profitablity. The prohibition served the United States as a powerful spur to the development of its own industrial revolution. At first the United States imported machines or copied them from English models, and then independently developed higher quality machines for its manufactures.[20]

Regarding borrowing modern technology, another significant lesson is provided by the Japanese experience. Most of the Japanese development was selfgenerated, but foreign influence had an important role to play. The Japanese closed their door to foreign investment until 1900 and learned Western technology on their own. The process was slow at first and entailed making many mistakes. After 1900 Japan began to accept foreign capital and influence, and its development strategy has effectively used both tariff protection and imported technology through licensing agreements.[21]

One of the factors that worked to the Japanese advantage in borrowing and adapting modern technology was the fact that Japan was the only country in Asia (and in Africa and Latin America) that escaped Western colonialism. Japan had a chance of independent national development.

Its being spared the mass invasion of Western colonialism saved it from the extremes of xenophobia which significantly retarded the spread of Western science and technology in Asia, Africa and Latin America. The exceptional Japanese receptivity to Western ideas and methods was largely due to the circumstance that Western science and technology were not associated in Japan with plunder, murder, inequality and racism as they were in the colonial territories. This circumstance permitted in Japan the creation of a socio-psychologial climate not inimical to the adoption of Western science and technology.[22]

The development of the Soviet Union is a unique experience in human history that deserves mentioning. The Soviet Union joined the ranks of leading industrialized countries in recent decades. The centrally planned economic system was one of the major contributory factors to the Soviet success.

An economic system is an important input along with the conventional inputs such as land, labor, and capital to the development process. It matters in observable and understandable ways as it is defined in a broad series of characteristics such as forms of property ownership, decision-making processes and relationship at workplace. As a result of the state control over savings and investment, the Soviet Union has been able to promote a rate of economic growth more rapid than would likely be possible in a free entreprise economy.[23]

It is misleading to attribute the Soviet achievement primarily to the system of central control. It needs to be mentioned that development is a gradual process and past experiences in Russia had succeeded in creating small but active nucleus from which further growth seemed assured.

Economic growth was already underway in Russia in the 1890's bringing to life modern coal, iron and heavy-engineering industries followed by the spread of technology to steel fabrication, chemicals and electricity. There was also substantial surplus in agriculture. It is true that Russia was the least developed European power in the late nineteenth century. But it was a developed power nonetheless, competing economically with some European states and possessing some modern industries well equipped with factories that used the most up-to-date Western models.[24]

Another late comer to the ranks of industrialized powers is the People's Republic of China. Here too, central control has played an important role, but the significance of past experience in providing a development nucleus is quite clear.

China could not achieve the technological and scientific levels reached by the West and Japan in the late nineteenth century. Some of the contributory factors to China's failure were China's conservatism; the decline of scientific inquiry; lack of substantial investment captial; and a tremendous population explosion, accompanied by a very low purchasing power that could not provide a stimulus to production.[25]

John Gurley, in his informative book, China's Economy and the Maoist Strategy, concludes that oppressed peoples elsewhere have to carry out their own revolutions in order to put themselves in a position to learn from China's development experience.[26] Besides the unique revolution that China had undergone, there is no doubt that early achievements have contributed to the recent progress.

For example, Chinese civilization made original advances in the arts, science, industry and agriculture, and Europe borrowed many of these inventions. Immensely important changes, refinements and creative contributions to human culture have continued in China for centuries. The Chinese were using elaborate water clocks six hundred years before one was independently invented in Europe. Water-powered amillaries were turning in China three hundred years before Copernicus; and the Chinese invented printing roughly five centuries before Gutenburg produced a movable type. Prior to the Industrial Revolution of the West, China's material culture was by no means inferior to that of any other country. In the thirteenth century, China reached a level of scientific knowledge unapproached in the West.[27]

In China, progress in agriculture took place long before it started in Europe. The evolution to annual cropping occurred at least a thousand years earlier while in Europe the shortening of fallow took place gradually during and after the Middle Ages. In China, two crops of rice and wheat a year were common before the sixteenth century representing a substantial technological progress in traditional agriculture.[28]

On the other hand, the situation in Ethiopia in the nineteenth century was by no means synonymous with anyone of the above countries. There was no demand for the new European technology nor was there a social class that could see profit in the new technology. The situation has not changed much since.

The commercial relations between European merchants and the imperial elites centered mainly on firearms. Hunting for elephants and captives could not create a demand for European technology other than firearms. For example, Tewodros was so much interested in the military technology of the West that he dismissed a corn mill as a useless invention. He thought that there would be nothing to do with the arms of women if machines were used to grind grain. Tewodros thus made his own cannons and mortars with the help of Protestant missionaries.[29]

Ethiopia's earlier trade contact with Europe did not help to introduce technical advances. In the first place, Ethiopia was totally isolated from Europe by the coastal establishments where most of Ethiopia's trade was conducted. Secondly, there were often hostilities between the coastal establishments and Ethiopia. Consequently outside influence could not reach inland. The coastal centers exported foodstuffs, ivory, and slaves from the interior that requried no technical innovations, and imported European goods whose demand was very small and limited to the elites.

During the reign of Menelik (1889-1913), contact with

Europe increased as many European entrepreneurs and self-employed concessioners entered Ethiopia. Menelik granted concession after concession to the Europeans, but put very little of the money to commercial and technical use. He put some of the European artisans at his disposal to improve his arsenals and royal workshops, but the influence of these Europeans did not extend beyond the palace enclosure.[30]

In Ethiopia, various artisan operations were long established and widespread, but the market and techniques of these activities were not developed. Prospective artisans lacked funds, better machines, equipment, techniques, managerial know-how, and incentives. The availability of imported alternatives further discouraged artisan activities. The technology embodied in the imported goods could not be used to improve internal markets and production techniques because of the inadequate skills and know-how of artisans.

The coming of modern industries in the post-war period was yet another threat to artisan operations in Ethiopia. Since the modern industries were not an extension of the artisan operations, some of the artisan activities declined while others disappeared completely. Such activities as weaving survived in the countryside while the modern industries held the urban centers employing mainly unskilled workers.

The emphasis placed in the mid-1960's on the expansion of import-substitution industries did not give Ehtiopia the technical capability to produce the needed products.

The domestic production of such consumer goods as confectionery, textiles, and leather footwear showed a significant increase. But consumer goods still made up a large portion of total imports due to lack of increased production in dairy products, soaps, cosmetics, wearing apparel, etc. In addition, import of wheat flour accounted for about a quarter of the total supply while flour mills operated below fifty percent of total capacity.

There was some increase in domestic production of intermediate goods, but about fifty percent was imported. Import-substitution of capital goods was virtually nonexistent and almost ninety percent of the needs were met by imports.[31]

## National Unity and Social Concensus

A strong and broad political base is necessary for a strong economic society. The existence of isolated areas of government, and fragmented markets were major obstacles to economic development in medieval Europe. Traveling merchants were subjected to different rules, regulations, laws, weights, measures, and money of various sovereignties. The creation of a unified market was one of the powerful contributory factors to England's emergence as the first great European economic power. The gradual centralization of power helped England enjoy an internally unified market. It needs to be mentioned also that the advantages of geographic space, richness of resources, and political unity made significant contributions to the development of the United States.

In the West, the building of a centralized nation-state took place in an atmosphere of deep national consciousness surpassing all other interests. The modern nation was formed when loyalty to country rather than to traditional authorities of dynasty and church became the primary political concern of all classes of society. The British experience of nation building is of vital importance to the rest of the world. There were certain essential elements that were responsible for the formation of the British nation-state.[32]

The English national consciousness was rooted deep in the past. As early as the middle of the sixteenth century, the English were imbued with a sense of national pride. By the seventeenth century, the basic elements of nationalism were already present in England. When feudalism was disintegrating in Europe, it was consolidated and civilianized in England, thereby inducing the formation of a territorially compact unit. A common language and literature were long formed to express the aspirations of the nation. There were common historical traditions and national heroes.

Another major quality of early British nationalism was its dedication to individual freedom. To the ideal of libertarian nationalism was added a most practical matter, parliamentary democracy which reflected a deep desire for a free society.

On top of the political factor, early British nationalism had social and economic dimensions. By the seventeenth century, the energetic middle class had accumulated great wealth and was seeking political power commensurate with its economic status. It was aware of its position in the society and consequently wanted to be free from the traditional restraints of monarchy, nobility, and clergy. The middle class identified its well-being with the well-being of the nation, and under its auspices national consciousness spread across the society.

The middle class was not alone in forming the nation-state. A sense of national consciousness filtered down from the middle class to both workers and peasants. As a result of the economic drives of the Industrial Revolution and the process of urbanization, the nation-state replaced the old forms of nationalism and provided for the masses a new source of security, and a motivation for an independent political activity.

English kings, too, became absorbed by national identity.

Realizing the tide of national consciousness, the kings maintained their power and interest by cooperating with the rising middle class against the feudal lords and cosmopolitan ecclesiastics.

A centralized nation-state was built on the basis of a coalition of political, military, and economic wings. There were coalitions of kings and urban middle class in Western Europe, of the samurai and the grain merchants in Japan, and of the commercial middle class and the more enterprising civil servants and soldiers in post-1860 Russia. These groups represented different motives and objectives, but shared one common, solid conviction: they all had a stake in the creation of an independent nation-state.

National consciousness appeared in a social order of mass education whereby love of country was inculcated among mostly illiterate Europeans at home and school.

The progressive values endorsed by most religions in the West created the right climate for economic activity, innovation, creativity and advancement. The Anglican Church showed little interest in the Great Unknown of the other world. It was an independent and a practical religion interested in all aspects of social life in England, especially in business activities and social welfare.

The English nation building process involved all classes of society. It was not a trickle down process by which a sense of national consciousness was imposed from the above. It was rather a widespread acceptance by all classes of society.

By the eighteenth century, England was the center of modern technology and a forward looking nation-state. Its modern technology and ideal of nation-state spread to the rest of the world. The American national consciousness was identified from its start with the ideal of individual freedom based on the English experience. The right to life, liberty, and the pursuit of happiness became the slogan of the new society.

Among the outstanding features of the American nationalism were a multi-ethnic character respecting diversity, and a spirit of egalitarianism resting on the equality of all citizens. While in Europe a person's social position tended to be fixed, in America there would be equality of status and social mobility. Any person could travel the road from poverty to riches and also back again. If class distinctions existed, they would be indeterminate and temporary.

Coming primarily from the middle and working classes of Europe, early Americans wanted a society with no vestiges of restrictive feudalism and manorialism. They wanted a nation in which careers would be open to talent and productivity, and a social consensus formed around the system of capitalism.

There is still a wide gap between reality and the democaratic ideals for some members of Western societies. For example, in the United States, despite the predominance of whites among the poor, the burden of poverty and economic disadvantages have been heavier on the blacks because of racial discrimination. Although public officials are ostensibly subject to the dictates of the majority, those with economic power and influence control much of the political process. Freedom of choice in the labor market is limited since blacks, other minorities, and women were excluded from high paying and rewarding occupations. In addition, because of the expenses of higher education and the importance of family contact and network, entry into high paying professions are becoming more and more dependent on the wealth of one's family.[33]

Western democracy is not yet complete. Barrington Moore defines it as a long and incomplete struggle to do three closely related things: to check arbitrary rules; to replace arbitrary rules with just and rational ones; and to obtain a share for the underlying population in the making of rules.[34]

In Ethiopia, popular nationalism of the Western type, does not exist. The concept of nationalism is as old as the country. Ethiopia has a traditional form of nationalism. Like in the West, the basic elements of nationalism have long existed in Ethiopia. There are the Tigre-Amhara culture and Christianity, a common language and literature, common historical traditions and national heroes, and finally, a territorial unit that had been effectively consolidated since the last quarter of the nineteenth century.

The traditional Christian nationalism of Ethiopia remained virtually unchanged for centuries. Individual freedom and independent political activity are unknown in Ethiopia. Little is allowed in the way of democratic rights. A parliament was established in 1931 but was under the direct control of the Emperor. The parliament represented the beginning of a revolution in social ideas in a country where noble birth had been the only consideration. The election of deputies provided the public with some sort of democratic experience. The parliament was abolished in 1975 by the Military Government, and Ethiopia became a Marxist-Leninist, one-party state.

Some writers believe that the parliamentary system is a wrong model for Africa.[35] But human beings, whether in Europe of Africa, are more alike than different. No matter where they live, they are subject to the same material, political and psychological needs. The argument that the parliamentary system is a false model for Africa is contemptuous.

It is too early to judge whether the system has succeeded in

Africa. "Rome was not built in a day." The parliamentary system emerged in England in the fifteenth century, and was not until the eighteenth century that it began to play an important role in the course of the English nationalism. The evolution of the English parliamentarianism was gradual, slow, and at times a discouraging process.[36]

It is argued that Africans are not wedded to the idea of parliamentary democracy, and the one-party system is seen as a return or continuation of traditional forms of "African democracy" in that it excludes the conception of an offical opposition of a majority and a minority. Opposition is said to be vital to the functioning of a developed plural democracy, but it is extremely difficult to mobilize people behind national objectives under such a system in the Third World. The argument runs that the one-party system is most suitable for preserving national unity, preventing the return of colonialsim, scotching the neo-colonialist endeavors and for developing the nation.[37]

In actuality, the one-party system has not provided a real democracy, national unity and economic progress in Africa. Because of, or in spite of, the one-party system abritrariness and repression still reign in Africa. What Frantz Fanon remarked in this regard is quite enlightening.

He said that the parliamentary system is faked from the beginning in many underdeveloped countries. The national middle class, economically powerless and unable to create a coherent society, chooses the single party system as an easy solution. Then the single party state imposes itself in a spectacular fashion making a display jostling and bullying the citizens. It proclaims, in the pretext of national unity, that the vocation of the people is to obey, and to be obedient till the end.

The party, Fanon said, which is supposed to make possible the free exchange of ideas, is transformed into a trade union of individual interests. Its mission becomes delivering to the people instructions which come from the summit. There is no give and take from the bottom to the top and from the top to the bottom which create and guarantee democracy in a party. The party is just a screen between the citizens and the leaders and helps the government to hold the people down.[38]

There are those who believe that the problems and exigencies of economic development provide the rationale for the tightening of political control in Africa. It is argued that a powerful, even ruthless government may be needed to begin the development process and cope with the strains of a successful development program. In the politically immature and unstable areas of the Third World, the exercise of leadership assumes the form of "strongman" government.[39]

It is true that development policies and programs are not eagerly accepted by all groups of society. And since a low income country has to plow back its surplus into capital formation for many years to come, even the lower social groups whose lot has improved because of the change are likely to feel a new resentment. This makes the task of political leadership more difficult in the Third World; and consequently requires the ability to provide impetus, inspiration, creativity, and work discipline rather that just being repressive and arbitrary.

Nation building in Ethiopia was primarily influenced by ethnic and religious elements. Suspicions and disparities have existed among the different groups. But Ethiopian politics has not been totally dominated by a single ethnic group. Emperors took persons from different ethnic groups and raised them to high positions at the state center rewarding them by office, rank, wealth and marriage. There were always coalitions of major ethnic groups at the center. But the Amhara, especially the Shawa elites, were favored over others.

The religious element of the Ethiopian nationalism was basic. The common people gave their support and loyalty to dynasty and the Axumite Christianity. The founders of Ethiopia accepted Christianity as early as the fourth century A.D. The Christian religion maintained cohesion of the people and linked them to their rulers. Axumite Christianity has been the main unifying ideology, especially in the Tigrai and Amhara plateau.

The Ethiopian nationalism was Christian nationalism in the typical sense of the term. There was often a smooth symbiosis between imperial rulers and the Church elites. The faithful sovereign always respected the positions of the Church elites and the clerics who preached loyalty to him and prayed for his longest life. In return the sovereign protected the interest of the Church by granting gult, expanding Christian learning and building religious institutions.

By the eighth century A.D., Islamic ideology and commerce became a unifying force in the lowland communities lying between the Red Sea and the plateau. Christians and Muslims often struggled for authority, revenue and territory for centuries. Finally Christian rulers contained Islamic pressure and extended themselves over the Muslim establishments. As a consequence, Christians dominated politics and government while Muslim Ethiopians controlled commerce.

Muslim Ethiopians were treated as outsiders and often suspected (for not good reason) of pursuing the interests of neighboring Islamic countries. While the Muslim elites enjoyed economic well being, they were locked out of the bureaucracy and political process. During Haile Selassie's Regime, it was declared that "Christians or Muslims, all are Ethiopians" and the bureaucracy was opened to Muslims and their religious practice tolerated.

With the coming of the military government, Church and State were separated; and Ethiopia became a secular state for the first time in history. Muslim holidays were declared national holidays. The separation of religion from government dethroned the Church from the political process, but religious fervor has gathered steam since, and the strong Christians do not seem impressed by the new ideology of Marxism-Leninism.[40]

It needs to be mentioned that the Church had played a significant part in the Ethiopian politics. Dynasty and Church had been the twin symbols of unity in Ethiopia for centuries. The Church was often the prime mover and instigator of rebellion against unpopular emperors, dissidents and foreign invaders.

The process of building centralized nation-state began in Ethiopia in the second half of the nineteenth century under Tewodros, followed by Yohannes and Menelik through an imperial system of government where the Church and the military played a key role. This system was later perfected and modernized by Haile Selassie.

There had been no common thread linking the various ethnic and religious groups held under the imperial system. Ethiopia does not have a strong middle class that can lead the creation of a popular national unity. The monarchy, nobility and clergy held the state against the productive groups for the growth of a middle class would threaten their positions built into the fabric of the imperial system. The problem of national unity was compounded by the high illiteracy rate, and many Ethiopians, especially those brought under the central control by the end of the last century, were new to the concept of national unity. The modern school system helped to inculcate Ethiopian nationalism but it came into existence just in the post-War period.

The coming of the Military Government has not paved the way for the growth of a strong middle class that can maintain influence over the society to promote progress and popular unity. The Military Government is not based on a coalition of forces and it has embraced Marxism-Leninism as a unifying ideology. But Ethiopia is not yet industrialized, and does not have a working class majority in the population for Marxism-Leninism to take roots.

During the imperial rule a number of groups (merchants, workers, peasants, professionals and ethnics) were excluded from the state, and had a common interest in the creation of a modern nation-state. But the formation of the new Marxist-Leninist state is not based on widespread involvement and acceptance of these groups. The interest of the various social groups of Ethiopia are much wider than that of Marxism-Leninism.

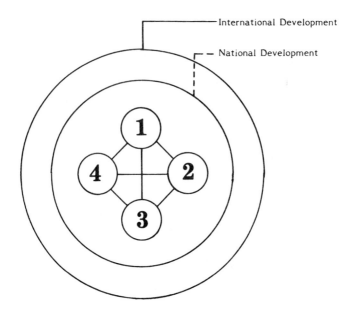

International Development

National Development

DEVELOPMENT DIMENSIONS

**1**

Agricultural Trans-
formation, Commer-
cial Advancement,
and Entrepreneurship

**2**

Work Ethic,
Equality of Status
and Social
Mobility

**3**

Scientific Inquiry,
Borrowing and
Adapting Modern
Technology

**4**

National Unity
and Social
Consensus

# 4

# Prospects for Development and Nation Building

## Internal Factors

Like the rest of Africa, Ethiopia has taken a long time as a subsistence economy. Much of Ethiopia's past was devoted to practicing undeveloped technical skills and professions. Development is at a very low stage and labor productivity is among the lowest in the world.

The prospect for economic development in Ethiopia depends on improving labor productivity by expanding technical skills and professionalism. It is essential to provide adequate incentives and opportunities to enterprising farmers, merchants, technicians, potential entrepreneurs and professionals who will eventually be able to produce innovations in all fields of science, technology, business management and leadership.

About eighty-five percent of Ethiopia's population live in rural areas relying mainly on subsistence crop and livestock economy. Agricultural modernization is an urgent task for improved living of the majority of the population and for overall economic development.

Improving agricultural productivity requires allowing enterprising farmers more scope and opportunity for permanent farming and independent experiments. In the West breaking up communal land into private farms, introducing major technical advances into agricultural implements and machines, and applying chemistry to agriculture resulted in a significant increase in agricultural production.

On the other hand, the Soviet Union created collective farms to modernized its agriculture. Relative to the West, the performance of the Soviet agriculture has been uneven. According to Soviet experts this is attributable to the Soviet system of agricultural organization, limited investment in agriculture. lower level of agricultural technology, and hostile climate making agriculture adaptation difficult.[1]

The Chinese modified the Soviet model of agricultural development to suit their conditions by creating communes in the rural areas.[2] But the Commune system is blamed by the post-Mao Regime for holding back the growth of farm output and a major change in the area of agriculture known as the responsibility or contract system has been introduced.

The essence of this innovation is to have each household become responsible for its own plot of land thereby stimulating individual initiative. Each household enters into a contract with the State to meet its minimum obligation. Whatever is produced in excess of the obligation remains the property of the household. Farmers are also encouraged to further enrich themselves by engaging in a variety of economic activities.[3]

The impact of private farm on incentive is demonstrated even in the Soviet Union where collective and state farms dominate the countryside. In the 1960's, private plots produced sixty percent of the total potato output, seventy percent of the total vegetable output, and thirty percent of the milk output. In the post-War period, the private plot sector accounted for forty percent of the family income on collective farms.[4] Despite ideological differences, the independent family farm seems to be the ideal system of farm organization for effective management, incentive, tenure and land improvement purposes.

The United States of America is one of the countries that benefitted the most from the family farm system. Agricultural modernization in the United States was based upon both historical experiences and local conditions.

Initially, the United States was settled as a nation of small farmers with the exception of cotton plantations in the south and cattle ranches in the west. Most of these farmers became owner-operators of family size farms ranging from forty to one hundred and sixty acres. Although bio-chemical technology has been introduced since the 1920's, plentiful land and scarce labor encouraged farm mechanization that swept the countryside after the Second World War. Labor productivity showed a remarkable increase, but on the other hand, increased mechanization and farm size expansion undermined the existence of the family farm system.[5]

In contrast, Japan - a country with a large rural population and a very limited amount of arable land - focused on increasing land productivity mainly through biochemical technology. In Japan land productivity is several times higher than that of the United States, but labor productivity in agriculture is still a fraction of the United States.

In Ethiopia a large portion of the population is concentrated in the rural areas. Independent landholder system was deeply rooted in Ethiopia although it had been underminded by an archaic land tenure system.

The main goal of the Ethiopian cultivator has always been to enjoy heritable and inalienable rights to hold and farm rist (ancestral land). Rist land provided livelihood to the peasant and was the basic means of asserting individual liberty.

A foreign traveler once said, "There is no harder worker than the Ethiopian peasant, and no more harmless and hospitable person when left alone and properly treated."[6] But the peasantry seldom enjoyed tranquility because of the constant pressure from the elites and their undisciplined associates who developed the taste to live on the labor of others.

Ethiopia is not yet a nation of technology-conscious farmers. The majority are tradition-bound, suspicious peasants, fearful of change that might jeopardize the slim margin yielding them life. The immediate question is how to transform peasant cultivators and migratory pastoralists into risk-oriented, technology-conscious small farmers.

The process of small farmer development requires a widespread diffusion of agricultural technology (bio-chemical and mechanical) through extension services.

In the late 1950's, technological improvements and extension services were considered the principal means of transforming agriculture in Ethiopia. Since the majority of the peasants had too small incomes to spend on agricultural improvements, small agricultural loans were initiated in the 1950's by the Development Bank of Ethiopia (now Agricultural and Industrial Development Bank). The benefits went only to those who could afford the collateral necessary to guarantee the loans. Those who did not own land could not benefit from the program. At any rate, the program did not succeed due to high service cost and default rates, and was discontinued by mid 1960's.

In the 1960's the Imperial Government encouraged the establishment of cooperative societies. Except in Bali, some kind of cooperative societies were formed in the other administrative regions. By the early 1970's, total membership of the cooperative societies reached 34,000 with a total capital of two million dollars.[7]

There were many impedements to the cooperative movement. Tenants were evicted if they joined cooperatives without the permission of their landowners; some cooperatives were controlled by landed elites who did not want to accept tenants and small landholders; credits were utilized mostly for mercantile activities rather than for agricultural improvement; interest rates were relatively higher on agricultural credits; relative to grain cultivators, industrial crop growers had the capacity to repay credits, thus the program benefited mostly the latter; in the absence of price support and marketing facilities, most of the producers were forced to sell their products immediately to meet their urgent needs; some members still borrowed from local moneylenders due to shortage of funds and had to deliver their products to the moneylenders instead of the cooperatives; trained staff, funds and membership training programs were seriously lacking; and finally, the cooperatives were opposed by merchants and traders because they assumed some of their activities.[8]

The extension services that began in the 1950's had only one hundred agents and thirteen supervisors for the whole country by the middle of the 1960's. In addition, the agents lacked funds and facilities to disseminate agricultural innovations.

By mid-1960's, the implementation of regional agricultural development policy, known as the "package program", began. It meant the establishment of agricultural production methods within geographically selected and limited areas in an effort to improve local farming through farmer participation. It was envisaged that if the agricultural innovations tried within the selected area were successful, they would be diffused to other areas as well by means of model farmers working under extension agents.

The first regional development project of its kind was the Joint Ethio-Swedish Chilalo Agricultural Development Unit (CADU) that began in 1967. CADU succeeded in increasing the income of its participants. But those who did not benefit from the program, such as traders, merchants and local elites, were opposed to CADU.[9] Now under the Military Government, CADU has been expanded and operates under the name of Arssi Development Unit (ARDU).

Most of the regional development programs of the 1960's and 1970's did not even get off the ground. They soon proved to be very expensive.[10] By 1971, the Imperial Government began the "minimum package" program to diffuse on a large scale some of the success experiences of the regional projects. The idea was to distribute farm inputs, implements, oxen and funds on credit to various groups of peasant cultivators.

Many farmers and cultivators were enthused by the program. Those who met the credit requirements were able to see the immediate benefit of the program. While others were interested to participate in the program, they were unable to pay the down payment, and landless tenants were frustrated by their landowners who refused to sign the credit contracts for them.[11] Institutional problems were the obdurate handicaps to be overcome in order to make the minimum package program a success in small farmer development.

By 1975, the land reform program of the Military Government removed the institutional problems and opened the avenue for the improvement of the vast majority of the population in the countryside. Despite the serious lack of technical and managerial skills and shortage of funds among the vast majority of the rural population, the Government embarked upon the expansion of collective and state farms rather than independent, small farms.

Local conditions and development of the rural population are primary in agricultural development. Ignorance about local conditions could defeat the best of intentions. Under conditions of rudimentary agriculture in Ethiopia, the human power and material bases essential for collective farms are virtually nonexistent.

Land reform is necessary for agricultural development, and it was long overdue in Ethiopia where land ownership had been at the heart of the political and economic processes. Land ownership accorded livelihood, security, power and individual liberty to the vast majority of the population. But ownership had been concentrated in the hands of a few individuals.

The land reform program of the Military Government abolished private property in land and replaced it by use rights.

Public ownership of land was seen as a solution to the concentration problem, but the reform program overlooked the historical significance of private ownership of land in Ethiopia and its impact on incentive.

The cornerstone of the agricultural policy of the Military Government was the Land Reform Proclamation of 1975.[12] It accorded the former landless tenants use rights to their existing holdings and farm implements until land redistribution would be carried out in the future. Rents, debts, and other obligations owed to landowners and all pending rural land cases were annulled in one stroke.

The Proclamation also granted use rights to those individuals willing to cultivate land by their own toil, and prohibited the hiring of farm labor by individuals, except by older people, widows and children who were unable to do farm work.

A farm family was allowed access to a maximum of ten hectares of land. The land was not to be sold, leased, mortgaged, or disposed of in any form, but its use rights were inheritable.

The Proclamation undoubetedly brought about a fundamental change in rural structure for the first time in Ethiopia. On the other hand, it did not capitalize on past experiences that were useful for agricultural development.

Some of the partnership arrangements among the ordinary cultivators were swept away along with the onerous tenancy relationships. Joint agricultural venture was undertaken among ordinary peasants to overcome shortages of land, labor, and capital and to supplement incomes.[13] One form of an agricultural partnership was where a peasant landowner contributed the land and half of the seeds, while the actual cultivator contributed the rest of the seeds, his own oxen and labor. The crops were divided in the field at harvest time; the cultivator's share varying from one-half to three-quarters of the crop. If the cultivator contributed an ox and the landowner supplied the other, the cultivator's share would drop from one-half to one-third.

Another joint venture was where a peasant landowner, who was an active farmer and had more land than he and his family could farm, would lease out his surplus land. Another situation involved shortage of capital in the form of plow oxen on the part of the landowner. A small or medium landholder usually owned an ox, and two such landholders pooled their oxen together to plow each other's land on alternate days. Furthermore, small landholders who owned some implements and oxen worked other's lands because they owned less land than they could farm with their labor and capital (oxen, implements, and seeds) to improve their incomes. They contributed their labor and capital, and paid between one-forth and one-half of their crops to the landowners.

Oxen are the most indispensable animals for agricultural production in Ethiopia. During and after the implementation of the Land Reform Proclamation, there was a serious shortage of oxen. In response to the Proclamation, the big landowners and better off peasants slaughtered or sold their cattle fearing confiscation. Consequently, a considerable number of cattle was withdrawn from agriculture. In some places, the shortage of animals was so critical that only a pair of oxen was available per four-peasant household.[14] The situation of plow oxen was worsened by the drought that drastically reduced the size of livestock.

The Proclamation provided also for the creation of a new rural organization, peasant association, covering a minimum area of eight hundred hectares—the same as the former chi-

qa-shum (village head) area. Some of the principal functions
of the peasant associations were redistribution of land, re-
solving conflicts over land, implementing land use directives,
establishing marketing and credit cooperatives, building
self-help projects such as schools, clinics, etc., in cooperation
with the Government and implementing rural development
programs.

The creation of peasant associations was rapid and successful in many parts of the countryside due to the commitment of
the Government and the accomplishments of the Development Through Cooperation Program. Peasant associations
played a very important role in consolidating power in the
countryside for the Military Government.

However, there was no adequate leadership in the countryside capable of carrying out the kind of responsibilities
assigned to the peasant associations. Furthermore, the associations were unable to establish and maintain new relations between better off peasants and former landowners on
the one hand and the rest of the peasantry on the other. And
this was not without consequences.

The big landowners retreated to the towns fearing the
excesses of the reform program, and with them went most of
the local moneylending system that had served the peasants
as a major source of credit. In some cases, the land abandoned
by landowners was left idle. Those who owned ten to twenty
hectares of land remained in the countryside if they belonged
to the same ethnic groups of members of peasant associations.
The Shawa settlers, most of whom were better farmers, had to
flee to the towns for their lives.

The previous chiqa-shum and abba-koro functions and new
responsibilities fell in the hands of inexperienced peasants in
the countryside. Most of the new leaders became authorita-

rian and began to enrich themselves through bribes and embezzling association funds.[15]

The process of small farmer development requires giving peasants security of tenure. Before the Land Reform Proclamation was implemented, most of the peasants had favored the idea of equal distribution of land and getting their shares registered under their names in the Government's tax books for reasons of security and protection.

The ultimate goal of the Proclamation was not to establish a private landholder system. Land redistribution was seen as a stage in the process of ultimate collectivization. Even then, the Government did not have adequate organization and personnel to smoothly administer land redistribution on a national scale. The political consequences of administering such a program was another matter. Thus, by 1976, the idea of land redistribution was abandoned and hardworking peasants were encouraged to cultivate extra land within the area of their associations. The question of security of tenure is still unresolved.

The coming of the land reform released tracts of land for the establishment of agricultural settlement schemes. The Military Government recognized the importance of settlement schemes for resettling drought victims and landless peasants drifting to the urban centers; and to create agricultural employment for the urban unemployed and for introducing nomadic pastoralists to secure, sedentary life.[16]

Settlement schemes began in Ethiopia in the 1940's when land was granted to war veterans and some landless peasants. While the peasant settlers worked their land, most of the other grantees sold their lands and pocketed the money or employed tenants to work for them. Most of the land distributed was disease-ridden and inaccessible.[17]

The number of settlement schemes increased very rapidly under the Military Government. The settlement schemes were created without allowing sufficient time for careful studies. Some of the sites were infested with tse-tse fly although the rainfall was adequate and the soils cultivable. The Government also turned some of the nationalized commercial farms into settlement schemes to save costs.[18] Most of the commercial farms nationalized were efficient and prosperous. Government interference in these farms soon resulted in drastic decline in output.

The success of settlement schemes depends on efficient management, member participation and an effective incentive system. Settlement schemes have to provide the settlers with adequate income, enabling them a secure living. Otherwise settlers will abandon the schemes in search of better opportunities. This problem was actually faced by some of the schemes created under the Military Government. While the migrant farm laborers and landless peasants showed great enthusiasm for access to farmland and agricultural activities, the urban unemployed abandoned their settlements in search of wage employment.[18]

The relationship between family and communal farms is another important factor that has to be settled in the process of agricultural organization. The competition between the two forms of agricultural organization for the peasants' labor and resources can impede agricultural production if left unresolved.

One of the responsibilities entrusted to the peasant associations was the promotion of cooperative production. Communal farms were created on adjacent lands abandoned by former landowners and helped peasants to extend their access to more land to grow additional crops. The peasants gave their primary attention to their family farms, and the communal farms were seen as supplements to the family farms. Communal farms accounted for an insignificant portion of the cultivated land in the countryside, and family farms were still the major source of income for the peasants.

Although cooperative production is seen as a useful means of mobilizing available resources for rapid development, it cannot be successful unless adequate technical and managerial capabilities are available in the countryside. Given the low level of development of the vast majority of the population in the countryside, cooperative production does not seem to be the ideal form of organization for agricultural improvement in Ethiopia. Furthermore, disparities in local conditions have to be considered in designing an agricultural organization.

Increased government involvement does not guarantee the success of cooperatives either. In Africa the failure of cooperatives has been attributed to much government control and lack of adequate planning and local involvement. It is suggested that cooperatives should be established gradually and carefully, thereby reducing government intervention and enhancing member education and participation.[19]

Ethiopia faces a much greater problem in transforming its livestock economy because of stubborn traditional practice of migratory pastoralism.

Cattle provide a way of storing wealth and mobilizing savings to pastoralists. In the pastoral economy, cattle are not raised for meat consumption as such. Pastoralists depend mainly on the by-products such as milk, butter and blood for their consumption and exchange. Sheep and goats provide a major source of meat protein. Cattle are also used for bride wealth payments, feasts and hospitality. Pastoralists are reluctant to butcher their major livestock and will go any length to avoid doing so. There are ecological reasons for this. Large herds are believed to have a viable core to survive droughts, diseases and other calamities.[20]

While cultivators in Ethiopia have some ideas about mixed farming, pastoralists are entirely herders with almost no practice of cultivation. Herders mostly inhabit the drier woodland and savanna areas as well as the steppe and semi-desert areas. In some areas herders reside among cultivators. The herders live in semi-permanent homes because of seasonal movements in search of pastures, water and markets.

Pastoralism is conducted on a communal basis. Membership in one of the corporate kin groups confers usufructory rights to all the range and water resources a member's herd needs. The exchange relation between pastoralists and cultivators is mutually beneficial. Migratory pastoralism has been the source of internecine conflict between the two groups. With the growth of population, the conflict over land has increased. As more and more land is put under cultivation, areas previously available for pastoralism diminished. Pastoralists have been confined to smaller areas, and overgrazing has caused land deterrioration and declining cattle productivity.

In order to transform the pastoral economy, the introduction of modern ranching practices and marketing systems are necessary. Commercial ranch operation requires abolishing communal pastures and seasonal movements; reducing herds to economic size in order to maintain a balance between resources and cattle population; and accepting the marketing concept, scientific stock breeding and range management practices. But these measures conflict with the traditional system. Through adequate price incentives, marketing infrastructure and education it is necessary to make commercialization gradually acceptable.

There cannot be a substantial and long lasting change in agricultural production without technical transformation. Land reform, even if it is most thoroughly carried out, does not represent agricultural advancement by itself.

By freeing most tenants from the onerous obligations and allotting plots of land to landless peasants and other oppressed groups, land reform may increase the incomes of the old and the newly created peasants. But this income is still low, and little if anything will be saved out of the increment. The improvement in the conditions of the peasants will be short-lived as the income increment will be wiped out by population growth. The situation of the peasants will decline to its previous level or below. In this sense then, land reform while temporarily improving the circumstances of the peasants, will depress aggregate output and eliminate the little agricultural surplus which hitherto existed for urban consumption, industrial processing and exports. There have been serious shortages of agricultural production and marketable surplus in Ethiopia since 1975 due to the structural changes brought about by the reform program.[21]

A substantial advancement in agriculture depends on the introduction of farm machinery, high-yielding varities, fertilizers, marketing services and infrastructure, price support, extension services, agricultural credit, water and soil conservation methods, and social services. Agricultural research is essential for developing various crops, sources of food, and suitable technology.

The introduction of farm machinery and implements is the most important factor for improving labor productivity. The conditions in rural Ethiopia favor the introduction of farm mechanization in stages.

The vast majority of the population live in the rural areas and large scale mechanization will cause massive displacement of labor. The non-agricultural sectors, at the same time, are too weak to absorb the displaced rural labor.

The rural labor is unskilled, and there is no technical capability to use sophisticated machinery and implements efficiently. There is surplus labor in the rural areas. The agricultural activity is seasonal with two peak periods of planting and harvesting. There are no other outlets in the countryside for the growing population. At this stage the introduction of improved implements and small machinery is essential to effectively use the rural labor and increase productivity.

In places where the introduction of big farm machinery is indispensable, it is necessary to incorporate the rural population into the development process, not just as wage earners on a seasonal basis but as permanent participants. In the past, large scale mechanization competed for land with the rural population but did not create sufficient opportunities for the displaced labor.

The promotion of fertilizer use is considered to be one of the major programs in agricultural development of the Green Revolution model. Fertilizer use is emphasized in agricultural development as it contributes to higher yields and other innovations such as improved seeds go with it.

In Ethiopia, fertilizer use was confined very much to large commercial farms and plantations. The widespread use of fertilizers by small farmers depends on farm credit, agricultural research and extension services, marketing infrastructure (access roads, storage, transportation, etc.) and price support.

The Green Revolution model of agricultural development is highly capital intensive and energy dependent. It requires adequate amounts of foreign exchange to import either chemicals or components to operate local factories.

Resource-efficient farming is a possible alternative to increase land productivity and employ more people in the rural areas. Over eighty percent of the total population in Ethiopia are engaged in agriculture, and the livestock size is among the biggest in Africa. Ethiopia has a great potential for improving its agriculture through composting and organic methods of farming. The utilization of manure, the introduction of leguminous crops and trees, interplanting and crop rotation can improve soil condition and meet food, fodder and firewood needs.[22]

The peasants in Ethiopia are not accustomed to fertilizing the soil with manure despite its abundance. Manure is mainly used for fuel. Kitchen garden plots around dwellings are cultivated with the help of manure and household wastes. Burning of soil, roots and weeds is widely used to fertilize the soil. It is also used to clear land for cultivation, to check the rapid growth of bushes, and to destroy rats and pests.

In the uplands, land is often terraced with dry-stone walls to reduce soil erosion. Soil erosion is a serious problem in Ethiopia due to a widespread rural mismanagement: overgrazing by cattle and wildlife on available vegetation; burning and clearing the land for agriculture; and cutting down trees and shrubs for fodder and firewood.

Ethiopia's woodlands are disappearing at a much faster rate than they are being replaced. The rapid decline in woodland has exposed the soil to erosion and created serious shortages of energy (firewood and charcoal). Ethiopia is one of the countries in East Africa along with the Sudan, Somalia and Kenya, vulnerable to serious drought and desertification. Combating these problems requires reforestations, soil and water conservation projects, irrigation agriculture, establishing new cattle routes and grazing patterns, constructing shelter belts, creating game reserves, and introducing drought-resistant plants.[23]

The drought problem is more urgent in northern Ethiopia where most of the region has turned into a wasteland because of sudden changes in climatic conditions and continuing deterioration of the supporting capacity of the land.

Another contributory factor to agricultural improvement is a farm price support system. Price support will create an equitable terms of trade for the flow of goods between the urban and rural areas. It will improve the incomes of farmers enabling them to buy better farm tools, machines, seeds, livestock, feritlizers, and other goods. At the same time, agricultural surplus for urban consumption and industrial processing will expand. Price support cannot be effective without adequate marketing infrastructure and distribution system.

The Military Government established an agricultural marketing corporation and a high price policy for grains in 1975 in order to increase production. The corporation purchased crops from farmers and operated retail outlets at the major markets. Farmers were able to benefit from the high prices, but there were still shortages of agricultural products that led to illegal markets and a strong upward pressure on retail prices.

Several factors were considered responsible for the problem. In the first place, the agricultural surplus hitherto extracted from the countryside by the former landowners was no longer forthcoming. Secondly, there was a conflict of interest between the marketing corporation and grain merchants—numbering from 12,500 to 25,000 in the rural areas and from 4,000 to 8,000 in towns—who were largely blamed for raising retail prices in terminal markets. Furthermore, increasing on-farm consumption was responsible for reduc - ing the size of the marketable surplus.[24]

Ethiopia's potential surplus for rapid industrialization lies in agriculture. When agricultural productivity is enhanced through improved farming techniques, part of the ensuing larger output per head must be saved for capital building. In the early stages of development, it is difficult to expect hungry peasants to do this voluntarily. The Government must create efficient mechanisms through taxation or investment plans to siphon off the surplus to support the capital accumulation process.

As labor productivity improves, the labor surplus hidden in the inefficient scale of agriculture can be diverted from agricultural pursuits to industrial and other pursuits in the rural and other sectors. The rural surplus labor can be employed in the construction of roads, dams, schools and clinics. But this construction cannot be carried out with bare hands. The capital building process needs a vast array of tools, equipment and machines by establishing a machine tool or capital equipment building sector. The immediate problem is the lack of technical capability on which industrialization critically depends, and in order to lay down the nucleus of a self-contained industrialization process, a pool of technical and managerial personnel has to be created.

Ethiopia's subsistence economy includes numerous people earning their living as small traders and artisans. The small traders mainly deal in foodstuffs and clothing thereby providing important outlets for peasant produce. They make small incomes from their operations and have limited capacity to invest in domestic markets and production techniques. The experiences and talent of this group can be tapped for further growth by creating incentives for small business development.

Various artisan operations were long established and

widespread in Ethiopia. The market and techniques of these activities were not developed. Artisan activities employ far more people than the modern industries.

The prospective artisans lacked funds, better machines, equipment and technical and managerial know-how. Their prosperity was hampered by lack of incentives. Unlike the modern industries, the artisan enterprises did not enjoy such incentives as tax holidays, preferential taxes and other subsidies from the government. They had to buy imported materials at high prices and were unable to turn out products at low costs to compete with imported alternatives. Due to tight credit policies and lack of adequate collateral, the artisan enterprises could not borrow funds to improve their techniques and markets.

The growth of commerce and crafts depends on providing merchants and artisans with adequate incentives and freedom. These two groups are important agents of development since they can create and expand innovations and opportunities. The state enjoys a monopoly of modern industries in Ethiopia, and enterprising merchants and potential entrepreneurs have been locked out of the industrial field.

Since 1975, the role of merchants has declined as state agencies and corporations assumed most of the activities of the private sector. With the growing importance of state enterprise, most of the foreign enterprisers who played key roles in commercial and artisan activities left the country, and the growth of potential entrepreneurs discouraged.

It is true that the merchant class in Ethiopia and the rest of Africa is not yet ready to tie its capital in its own factory development and certainly lacks political experience in government. Relative to the merchant class in Asia or elsewhere in the Third World, the African merchant class is a much newer class.

In India, before 1947, there were already large factory-owning groups of Indian capitalists such as Tata and Birla who were beginning to spread their links both vertically and horizontally, securing a strong position in entire industries and extending their influence through a whole range of enterprises. In China, prior to 1949, there were Chinese capitalists owning large factories such as the textile factory owners in Shanghai.

Besides the weak merchant class, the problem facing African countries has been the lack of cooperation from the outside world to finance projects that can strengthen economic independence. The new African states have found it necessary to look towards the state sector of the economy as an important means of development.[25] It is believed that public enterprise system will speed up economic development and make the African economies more national.[26]

In spite of, or because of, the public enterprise system, rapid industrialization has not occurred in Africa. Although public enterprise is intended to fill the gap created by a weak merchant class, it has been unable to provide innovative entrepreneurship that is essential for rapid economic growth. If Ethiopia is to be modernized, it needs to build a strong merchant class that is dedicated to the advancement of production techniques and internal markets.

## External Factors

The existence of internal possibilities and opportunities is primary for a development process to get under way in Ethiopia. But Ethiopia cannot develop without the industrialized countries and the industrialized countries cannot further grow without Ethiopia. There is mutual benefit in economic development.

One of the contributory factors to Ethiopia's failure to achieve economic development and technical progress was its inaccessibility and isolation. Ethiopia needs to encourage a wider contact and inflow of ideas, and maintain institutional flexibility for its internal development.

External trade offers capital and technology for development. Ethiopia can benefit effectively from external trade if it is selective in its demands for world products and technology. Although Ethiopia's export earning and purchasing power are still low, it needs to utilized its current earnings efficiently by restructuring its demand for foreign goods and techology based on urgent development priorities.[27] This will release funds for productive purposes and eventually raise income.

Foreign capital can play a significant role in internal development. But despite the inflow of foreign capital, many African countries have not improved their situation, and are now on the brink of bankruptcy. There are two different explanations for this problem. One attributes the problem to inadequate trade and exchange rate policies while the other holds the open trade policy itself responsible.[28]

Both views do not adequately explain the problem. Foreign capital for business as well as political reasons has gone for ambitious and hectic government projects. The lending policies of international development agencies are not geared to creating and strengthening internal capabilities by extending loans and capital directly to productive groups.

The International Monetary Fund (IMF) sees Africa's economic crisis from a standpoint of over-valued currency that hampers export earnings and debt financing potentials. The IMF "medicines" are devaluation which will reduce the demand for imports and stimulate exports; reduction of domestic demand by cutting government expenditures and/or increasing tax; and imposing tight wage controls to ensure that both prescriptions work effectively.

The conditions for the IMF "medicines" do not exist in many Third World countries. Two conditions have to be in place for the IMF prescription to work. First, there has to be a well developed productive capacity that can respond to the challenges and opportunities provided by the "medicines", and secondly, a welfare system to minimize the hardships arising from industrial restructuring. In the absence of a developed productive capacity, the IMF prescriptions cannot be effective.

In Africa, production structures are undeveloped and inflexible. By raising the cost of imports, devaluation makes it more difficult to overcome the constraints and rigidities of productive capacity, and a secular deterioration of terms of trade becomes inevitable.

Devaluation adds to inflationary pressure at home thereby worsening the unequal distribution of income and limiting internal markets. Trade liberalization under the present conditions further weakens domestic industries by creating undue advantage for transnational corporations. Finally, the reduction in public spending leads to drastic cuts in the much needed areas such as health and education.[29]

The so-called overvalued currency is not the correct point of departure to understanding the real problem in Africa. After a painful experience with the IMF prescriptions, Michael Manley, the former Prime Minister of Jamaica, rightly concluded that the problem in the Third World is not the search for markets for sophisticated wheat farmers already capable of high levels of productivity, but how to get a simple peasant to become an efficient producer in the first place.[30] That task is well beyond the range of conventional tools of the neo-classical, monetarist approach of the IMF on which many development programs are based today.

Opportunities for stimulating internal development can be sought also in foreign economic aid. Africa that began receiving foreign assistance about a quarter of a century ago is more dependent now than ever on aid goodwill. This is an indication that foreign assitance has not gone for the growth of farmers, merchants, technicians and other professionals who have direct contact with the physical process of production.

The World Bank estimated that a doubling of foreign economic aid to Africa by the end of the 1980's (from $4.9 to $17.9 billion in current prices) could lead to an average annual per capita growth rate of 2.5 percent during the remainder of the decade.[31] But what is more important is to make aid funds accessible to productive groups who need them most.

The United States gives aid to African regimes that maintain stability (status quo), strengthen U.S. economic presence, and respond to ideological sympathy and support the U.S. on international issues.[32] These criteria cannot create economic and political opportunities for the growth of productive groups in Africa.

Because of the influence of domestic and international politics on aid appropriation, the United States regards Africa at the bottom of its international priorities. Africa receives less than fifteen percent of the total foreign aid. This is less than what Asia and Latin America receive, and far less than the Middle East.[33]

The issue is not that increasing U.S. aid will create progress in Africa, but that aid should be used for constructive purposes. If aid is used for the purpose of creating a client state, it will waste the resources of both donor and recipient countries. Aid is not just a free gift. It helps promote export industries of the donor country and provides development capital to the recipient country. Productive use of this capital can be ensured if it is used in assisting the growth of internal markets and production techniques of the recipient country, and thereby raise the income of the people. Foreign aid needs to be channeled directly to farmers, merchants, technicians and other professionals.

The present U.S. policy has little to do with Africa's internal situations. The main goals of the policy are pursuing short-term economic interests and maintaining balance of power. The United States has failed to address the issue of apartheid in South Africa, the struggle for independence in Namibia, and above all, economic development in Africa.

Such factors as poverty, political repression, colonialism and apartheid can set political forces in motion and may well lead to that very disruption in the power balance in Africa. Even if a balance of power is neatly organized, it will not ensure peace by eliminating the causes of war unless it addresses internal conditions at their sources.

Soviet involvement in Africa has been shaped by indigenous conditions. It is easy for the Soviet Union to get involved in Africa since various internal struggles challenging the status quo are in process. The Soviets provide funds and arms in return for benefit and influence. However, they have not succeeded in penetrating an area and establishing permanent power position.[34]

The competition among the superpowers for world influence is a mixed blessing. It presents both opportunities and dangers for the Third World; there are opportunities in the economic field, but the military and geopolitical competitions are inimical to the Third World development.

The African countries face formidable external forces in their struggle for independence and economic development.

These struggles present a problem to both superpowers. In as far as they are against the status quo, they confront directly the United States. They represent a threat at the same time to global equilibrium which the Soviet Union tends to preserve under the rule of peaceful co-existence.[35]

It is difficult for a small nation to pursue a non-aligned course of development. In their quest for peaceful coexistence, the superpowers try to eliminate neutralism. For example, Yugoslavia faces increasing difficulties in relation to both superpowers in maintaining its non-aligned status; Cyprus was invaded by Turkish troops and its neutrality was destroyed; and Jamaica, under Michael Manley, failed to pursue its own "third path" of development.[36]

Western countries and the two superpowers are actively present in resource-rich Africa. No clear rules of behavior have been developed to limit the action of the superpowers in Africa. The main problem in Africa as in the Middle East is disunity which is fomented by a multitude of internal and external forces as well as superpower conflicts.[37] Unity within and among African countries is therefore essential for stability and economic development. It is true that no revolution or development process can succeed without foreign alliance. But dependence on foreign power can be minimized by strengthening internal unity and regional cooperation.

## Popular National Unity

If Ethiopia is to become modernized, it needs to achieve a popular national unity. The process of national unity is a long and difficult task. It took the European and American states, supposedly possessing more political sophistication, several centuries before achieving the blessing of peace and security. The West learned the road of national unity by bitter experiences to which the unification of Germany and Italy and the American Civil War bear testimony.

Ethiopia does not have a democratic tradition and independent political activity. It had been ruled for centuries like a Machiavelli's polity: with emperor, aristocracy, palace intrigues, church and strong army, built on an utterly wretched peasanty.

The sovereign was regarded as the elect of God and an embodiment of innate wisdom and divine power to rule: "God not people can elect their ruler." Most of the elites were self-centered, callous and contemptuous in their treatment of the common people beneath them.

Obedience to elders and superiors without any question is looked upon as the only correct method of regulating human relations and creating harmony in the society. Independence and freedom of dissent are unkown. Dissent is considered a heresy, and dissenters are given the severest punishment. It is only through conspiracies that changes are attempted.

The most significant attempt took place in 1960 as a result of an alliance between progressive military and civilian intellectuals rallying behind the agrarian question. Although the attempt was unsuccessful, it opened a new chapter in the political history of Ethiopia by creating political awareness in the minds of the people and suggesting a modern political process as an alternative to the traditional order.[38]

Rule of democracy has been denied to the Ethiopian people. The people have no voice in government. Little has been allowed in the way of democratic rights. The Parliament, created in 1931, merely served as a rubberstamp institution under the control of Haile Selassie, and no political parties were allowed. Party politics began in Eritrea in the 1940's. But the annulment of the federal system in 1962 suppressed the Eritrean political parties and denied the rest of Ethiopia the opportunity of modern means of political organization. Blinded by self interest, the imperial elites left the Ethiopian people in political darkness relying only on a strong army as their solid base of power and means of maintaining unity.

As the country was thrown into chaos and anarchy by economic crisis and famine, the military emerged in 1975 as Ethiopia's only "party" with organized strength sufficient to overthrow Haile Selassie's Regime and to determine the course of Ethiopia's future. In the absence of any kind of political organization, the military assumed the historical role of political leadership of Ethiopia after Haile Selassie.

Under the military leaders, Ethiopia began the one-party system when the Worker's Party of Ethiopia was launched in September, 1984.[39] The rest of Africa started this system earlier, but the one-party system has not provided real democracy, national unity and economic progress in Africa.[40]

The one-party system monopolizes political decision and administrative functions in the hands of the elites at the state center, turns the various branches of government and free press into instruments of the party, and eliminates oppostion.[41]

There can be no unity without allowing diversity. A nation is free when there is individual liberty to make conscious judgment.

The West did not master the multi-party system in one day. It was a process that has been learned over centuries. It is unreasonable to expect Africa to accomplish in a couple of decades what has taken Europe and the United States hundreds of years.

In the West, unity was achieved when the modern nation-state emerged as the satisfier of the material, political and security needs of all individuals. In Ethiopia, popular unity will depend on the creation of a nation-state that will satisfy the various needs of all classes of society.

Patriotism in Ethiopia had been equated with loyalty to emperor and country; Christianity served as a unifying ideology. This has been replaced by a new patriotism: loyalty to country (Ethiopia First) and the Revolution since the military takeover. Marxism-Leninism is the offical doctrine and unifying ideology. The new patriotism was consummated with the establishment of the Ethiopian Worker's Party to which all groups and sectors of the society have to give loyalty. But winning loyalty, and popular unity, depends on the fulfillment of the interests of the different groups and sectors which are much wider than that of Marxism-Leninism.

Ethiopia is made of diversity and has to learn to live with it. There are no other alternatives to this but to respect equally the diverse ethnic groups, interest, beliefs and ideas in the interest of popular national unity.

Ethiopian intellectuals have to turn to and draw strength from in-depth studies of their own people and country. It is an urgent task of Ethiopian intellectuals to provide the theoretical content of a binding nationalism and to seek   the truth in their respective fields of competence without ideological bias. There is no absolute or singular truth. The pursuit of new ideas has to be tolerated and encouraged. Development is a creative process. Creativity will not grow if individual freedom and knowledge are restricted.

Friendly relations with the neighboring countries can lead to regional cooperation for economic development and stability in Ethiopia. While there is a great potential for such cooperation in northeast Africa, Somalia's desire of territorial expansion and outside interference in the Eritrean conflict have dampened the prospect.

African elites, like the European elites in early nationalism, are not sitting down at conference tables and working
out the destiny of their countries. Instead, they resort to
military force and waste resources and human lives.

The Eritrean conflict cannot be resolved without considering the economic and security interest of the Ethiopian State,
and the right of the Eritrean people to conduct their own
internal affairs. On the other hand there is no historical
justification for Somalia to claim the Ogaden region which
was incorporated into the Ethiopian Empire during the
Scramble for Africa, and in point of fact, before the creation of
a Somali state. "Greater Somalia" was a British colonial
design which has been exploited by the Somali rulers since
1960.

In the absence of peace and cooperation in Ethiopia, resources will continue to be diverted from development to war
needs. Rebel activities in the northern famine zones are sapping the
government's energy and hampering relief operation.[42] The famine
provides a basis for rebellion and political opposition. It was one of the
major factors that set political forces in motion and brought about the
downfall of Halie Selassie. The survival of the Military Government is
now being tested by the same problem.

Famine is not confined to Ethiopia alone. Because of two to
three years of no rain, some twenty-five African countries are
in a famine list, among which four countries (Ethiopia, Chad,
Mauritania and Mozambique) are without any food, to feed
their starving peoples.[43]

The tragedy cannot be averted by Africa alone. It requires
mobilizing outside assistance by the African countries, other
governments, and international agencies. Ethiopia is the
hardest hit by this tragedy, and if the drought continues and
outside assistance is not forthcoming, some six to seven million Ethiopians will face death by starvation.

The decline in Ethiopia's food production and escalating superpower conflict have contributed to the complexity of the famine problem in Ethiopia. In the meantime, the famine has claimed the lives of millions of people, mostly children, leaving the region without a future generation.

The people of northern Ethiopia took pride in independence and self-reliance and had supported swarms of rentiers for centuries. They are now faced with the worst famine in history.

In the short run, the main focus should be to strengthen the relief operation in order to save as many lives as possible. The situation can improve if the rain resumes. In the long run, the supporting capacity of the region has to be restored through careful planning and implementation of reforestation, soil and water conservations, irrigation and transportation schemes, as well as the establishment of weather research, information and distribution systems.

In Ethiopia, the horrendous task of economic development and nation building still lies ahead. The removal of the traditional elites from authority in 1975 created the preconditions for rapid progress toward modernization in Ethiopia. However, their removal from authority by itself does not guarantee progress. The prospect for Ethiopia's modernization depends on generating capital and leadership for development and dealing with formidable world forces, and on creating a democratic political process that can give birth to a new, cohesive society, devoting itself to the development of its **productive** resources and that can provide all the people of Ethiopia with adequate voice and share in the sovereignty and wealth of their country.

# 5

# Conclusion

The existing theories of economic development have enriched our understanding about the lack of development in the Third World. However, they do not explain adequately the lack of development in the Third World, particularly in Ethiopia.

The mainstream development doctrine helps us identify some of the critical problems of Third World countries. But it believes that the problem in the Third World is insufficient spread of capitalism, and the solution to the problem is a more thorough penetration of capitalism.

The mainstream doctrine emphasizes disciplinary, mechanical aspects and ignores specific conditions of the Third World as well as the negative impacts of external forces on internal development. By treating economic development as the result of outside forces, it ignores the historical dimension of economic development and denies the Third World a history of its own.

The mainstream school is rightly concerned with the impact of national unity on economic development and states that a positive correlation exists between economic development and nation building. Thus, increasing national unity is equated with modernity. It ascribes the lack of national unity in the Third World to ethnic heterogeneity.

The neo-Marxist-Leninist school radically departs from the notions of the mainstream doctrine treating the lack of development in the Third World as the product of the same historical process that created the development of the capitalist world. It believes that socialism and disengagement from the capitalist world are essential and indispensable conditions for attaining economic progress and ending dependency in the Third World.

By treating economic development from a historical dimension, the neo-Marxist-Leninist doctrine gives us a valuable insight into the process of development. However, it emphasizes imperialism of the capitalist system as the primary cause for the lack of development in the Third World, and fails to address adequately the productivity of labor as the essence and key to economic development.

The neo-Marxist-Leninist doctrine directs our attention to the impact of imperialism of the capital system on nation building in the Third World. Most of the nations in Africa were carved out by Western powers. Yet, the doctrine still considers the independent countries in Africa as colonial or neocolonial countries and attributes the lack of national unity in these countries to imperialism of the capitalist system. While underestimating bourgeois democracy, it fails to explain how full democracy and popular unity can be achieved under the so-called "democratic centralism" or "working class dictatorship."

The lack of development in Ethiopia is attributable to the low productivity of labor, which in turn is caused by the low level of technical skills and professionalism. On the other hand, because the essential elements of popular unity are absent, political instability has made economic dedelopment a difficult process in Ethiopia.

There is no simple set of features that can explain the processes of economic development and nation building. The historical experience of the industrialized countries is of great significance for the purpose of analyzing the problem and prospects of economic development and nation building in Ethiopia.

One of the factors essential for economic development is a successful and thorough transformation of subsistence agriculture into commercial farming. This process requires the introduction of major technical and biological advances in agriculture by departing from the traditional farming practices and land use patterns. Ethiopia's agricultural practices and implements have remained virtually unchanged for centuries.

Another contributing factor to technical innovations and economic growth is an advancement in commerce and entrepreneurship. Ethiopia has not been a trading economy. After Axumite Ethiopia lost control of the Red Sea trading routes by the eighth century A.D., Ethiopia remained isolated until very recently, lying far beyond the horizon of Europe.

Key commercial and artisan activities were in the hands of foreign residents who often felt insecure working under the pressure of the imperial elites, and preferred to invest their profits abroad rather than at home. Native merchants emerged in the 1940's, but they were still trade-oriented rather than production-minded to contribute to technical innovations.

In Ethiopia, investment in manufacturing and key trading activities has remained a state monopoly hampering the development of commercial talents and technical skills. This process has discouraged the growth of potential entrepreneurs.

In order for economic development to occur, the majority of the population have to identify with technological progress and should not disdain contact with the physical process of production. In Ethiopia, the people have not learned the economic attitudes that foster rapid industrialization.

Business or production-oriented careers are looked upon with scorn. Work is not deemed an absolute value; commerce and crafts are despised, and relegated to "inferior" groups. Status is ascribed rather than achieved by ones own hard work. The value system minimizes the importance of material rewards and economizing. The avenue to upward mobility has been through bureaucratic work rather than productive activities. As a result, members of the various productive groups are held down.

The spirit of scientific inquiry is one of the main features associated with technical advance and economic growth. In Ethiopia, tradition still dominates the thought pattern. Modern education began just in the 1940's, and scientific inquiry is a fairly recent phenomenon. The modern intelligentsia is small, young, and disunited; institutional facilities very limited; and academic freedom conducive to arriving at new truths is virtually nonexistent.

Economic development can occur by borrowing and internalizing modern technology. For example, in the last quarter of the nineteenth century, Europe, North America and Australia were able to develop with British influence. Japan borrowed and domesticated Western technology at the same time. Economic development proceeded rapidly in these places and in some of them soon surpassed that of England since progress had been already under way and internal capabilities to learn modern technology available before the coming of British influence.

The Soviets joined the ranks of leading industrialized nations in recent decades. The People's Republic of China is another newcomer to the ranks. In both countries state control over the economy was a contributory factor to rapid economic growth. Communism succeeded in the Soviet Union and the People's Republic of China because of past experiences that had created active technical and professional nucleus for further growth.

The situation in Ethiopia, on the other hand, is by no means synonymous with any one of the above. Ethiopia has not been a progressive economy. It does not have the internal capabilities to borrow and domesticate modern technology. Foreign investment comes to Ethiopia not in response to a development process already under way, but rather in anticipation of future development.

The emergence of a popular unity has a significant impact on economic development. This requires dedication to individual liberty, representative democracy, energetic middle class, coalition of all classes of society, and mass education to inculcate love of country and a deep sense of national consciousness.

Ethiopia does not have a democratic tradition. Human relation and social harmony are maintained by emphasizing obedience to elders and superiors. Its middle class is small and young, and the majority of the population are illiterate. Individual liberty and independent political activities are unknown. Political and administrative decisions have been monopolized by elites at the state centers, and there is a huge gap between elites and non-elites.

Traditionally, the people gave loyalty to emperor and country. The sovereign was regarded as an embodiment of innate wisdom and divine power.

In 1975, the traditional forms of authority were removed by the military and loyalty to a Marxist-Leninist Party became the new patriotism. Ethiopia is not industrialized and does not have a working class majority in its population for Marxism-Leninism to take roots as a unifying ideology.

Ethiopia is made up of diverse groups whose interests are much wider than the interest of Marxism-Leninism. The involvement of all groups and classes of the society at the state center is essential for popular unity to occur.

The prospect for economic development in Ethiopia depends on expanding technical capabilities and professionalism to improve labor productivity. It is necessary to provide adequate incentives and opportunities to productive groups who will eventually produce innovations in all fields of science, technology, business management and leadership.

In order to improve agricultural production, the subsistence crop farming and livestock rearing practice need to be replaced by individual owner-operator farms allowing enterprising farmers more scope and opportunities for permanent farming, independent experiments in scientific agricultural improvements and sedentary stockbreeding.

The development of commerce and crafts requires providing merchants and artisans with adequate incentives and opportunities of upward mobility. A strong merchant class is essential for providing innovative entrepreneurship for rapid economic growth. This indispensable role cannot be played by state enterprises alone. Individual initiative in all fields of production has to be encouraged in order to expand technical skills, professionalism, and leadership.

The existence of internal opportunities are primary for economic development to occur in Ethiopia. External factors can play a positive role if they are geared to developing internal capabilities. Ethiopia needs the outside world, and the outside world needs Ethiopia. Thus, Ethiopia has to maintain institutional flexibility in order to attract and make the best of use of external opportunities for internal development.

With the removal of the traditional elites in 1975, the preconditions for rapid industrialization were created. But this does not guarantee progress by itself. If Ethiopia is to become modernized, it has to generate capital and leadership for development and dealing with formidable international forces, and establish a democratic political process that can provide all the people of Ethiopia with adequate share in the sovereignty and wealth of their country.

APPENDIX 1

Annual Inpayments and Outpayments on Foreign Investments in Ethiopia

(in millions of Ethiopian dollars), 1960-1974

| Year | Inpayments | | | Outpayments | | | Net Inpayments/Outpayments(-) | | |
|---|---|---|---|---|---|---|---|---|---|
| | Loan | Direct Invest. | Total | Loan | Direct Invest. | Total | Loan | Direct Invest. | Total |
| 1960 | 24.7 | 19.8 | 44.5 | 3.3 | 9.6 | 12.9 | 21.4 | 10.2 | 31.6 |
| 1961 | 18.7 | 10.4 | 29.1 | 4.8 | 14.4 | 19.2 | 13.9 | - 4.0 | 9.9 |
| 1962 | 65.9 | 8.0 | 73.9 | 6.4 | 5.4 | 11.8 | 59.5 | 2.6 | 62.1 |
| 1963 | 50.8 | 26.3 | 77.1 | 13.7 | 6.6 | 20.3 | 37.1 | 19.7 | 56.8 |
| 1964 | 23.0 | 23.6 | 46.6 | 13.9 | 6.4 | 20.3 | 9.1 | 17.2 | 26.3 |
| 1965 | 61.6 | 26.0 | 87.6 | 16.4 | 8.8 | 25.2 | 45.2 | 17.2 | 62.4 |
| 1966 | 77.8 | 22.8 | 100.6 | 21.7 | 8.6 | 30.3 | 56.1 | 14.2 | 70.3 |
| 1967 | 52.3 | 11.7 | 64.0 | 26.3 | 10.0 | 36.3 | 26.0 | 1.7 | 27.7 |
| 1968 | 86.3 | 6.5 | 92.8 | 31.3 | 10.5 | 41.8 | 55.0 | - 4.0 | 51.0 |
| 1969 | 73.3 | 2.3 | 75.6 | 35.8 | 9.5 | 45.3 | 37.5 | - 7.2 | 30.3 |
| 1970 | 73.8 | 5.8 | 79.6 | 42.3 | 11.5 | 53.8 | 31.5 | - 5.7 | 25.8 |
| 1971 | 119.3 | 7.0 | 126.3 | 43.0 | 10.8 | 53.8 | 76.3 | - 3.8 | 72.5 |
| 1972 | 88.3 | 9.8 | 98.1 | 36.5 | 17.5 | 54.0 | 51.8 | - 7.7 | 44.1 |
| 1973 | 82.3 | 47.3 | 129.6 | 35.1 | 18.0 | 53.1 | 47.2 | 29.3 | 76.5 |
| 1974 | 78.3 | 38.7 | 117.0 | 31.8 | 21.3 | 53.1 | 46.5 | 17.4 | 63.9 |

Source: Computed from IMF, Balance of Payments Yearbook, Vol. 14, 1957-61; Vol. 19, 1962-66; Vol. 24, 1967-71; and Vol. 27, 1967-74.

APPENDIX  II

Annual Direct Foreign Investment in Ethiopia
(in millions of Ethiopian dollars)

1960-1974

| Year | Reinvestment of Undistributed Earnings | Direct Investment From Abroad | Total |
|------|------|------|------|
| 1960 | 3.8 | 19.8 | 23.6 |
| 1961 | 4.2 | 10.4 | 14.6 |
| 1962 | 5.1 | 8.0 | 13.1 |
| 1963 | 4.7 | 26.3 | 31.0 |
| 1964 | 6.7 | 23.6 | 30.3 |
| 1965 | 1.1 | 26.0 | 27.1 |
| 1966 | 3.7 | 22.8 | 26.5 |
| 1967 | 2.8 | 11.7 | 14.5 |
| 1968 | 5.5 | 6.5 | 12.0 |
| 1969 | 4.5 | 2.3 | 6.8 |
| 1970 | 4.0 | 5.8 | 9.8 |
| 1971 | 7.3 | 7.0 | 14.3 |
| 1972 | 12.5 | 9.8 | 22.3 |
| 1973 | 17.5 | 47.3 | 64.8 |
| 1974 | 21.3 | 38.7 | 60.0 |

Source: Computed from IMF, Balance of Payments
Yearbook, Vol. 14, 1957-61; Vol. 19, 1962-66; and
Vol. 27, 1967-74.

APPENDIX III

# A Historical Account of the Ethiopian Social Formation

## Axumite Ethiopia

It is an indisputable fact that the origin of Ethiopia was the ancient Kingdom of Axum (in present-day Tigrai). The rulers of Axumite Ethiopia supported themselves by controlling the trade routes of the African Red Sea coast. They supplemented their incomes with booty and tributes collected from the regions lying north and westwards of Axum as fas as Meroe. Working in good terms with the Greco-Egyptian merchants, Axumite Ethiopia established commercial relations with the Byzantine power as early as the first century A.D. The trading establishments along the trade routes and the coastal towns settled by Yemenites, Jews, Egyptians and Greeks, who controlled the Axumite commerce, flourished. Following in the footsteps of commercial and maritime relations with Greco-Egypt, Christianity entered Axumite Ethiopia in the fourth century A.D.

During the first six centuries, Axumite Ethiopia enjoyed a remarkable prosperity. The material relic (obelisks of Axum) left behind is testimony to the degree of security, wealth, creative boldness and technical skill attained by the Axumites during this period.

## Islamic Commerce and Ideology

A big break in the development of Axumite Ethiopia occurred in the eighth century A.D. owing to the expansion of

Islam. The Red Sea trading stations were either destroyed (Adulis) or occupied (Massawa and Dahlak Islands) by Arab traders and colonists.

By securing the coastal bases, the Arabs cut off the Axumites from the Red Sea, organized under Islam nomad tribes such as the Beja and Saho, living between the Sea and the plateau, and turned them against Christian Ethiopia. As a consequence, the Axumites lost control of the sea routes. Most of the merchants who populated the coastal and trade route settlements left as central control weakened and the trade routes became dangerous and inaccessible. Eventually, the sea commerce of Axumite Ethiopia collapsed and its coinage became worthless.

In the succeeding centuries, Axumite Ethiopia turned its face to the inaccesible fertile regions of south and southwest. It focused on the mountainous regions of Lasta, Amhara (present-day Wallo), Shawa and Gojjam to pursue austere development and Christian learning.

After securing the coastal bases and organizing nomad tribes, the Arab colonists began their first phase of systematic penetration of northeast Africa between the tenth and twelfth centuries. It was at this time that eastern Shawa and the Sidama "states" were penetrated. Muslim establishments dotted the periphery of Ethiopia from Suakin to the east of Shawa on the fertile uplands of Ifat.

During the period of the Zagwe Dynasty (1137-1270) of Christian Ethiopia, eastern Shawa (Ifat) became the center of an Arab Dynasty: Makhzumi (Walasma). The Muslim population of the Sultanate of Ifat (Jabara or Jabarta) cultivated banana and sugar cane on their fertile land. The rulers of Ifat prospered through commerce and by controlling the trade routes, linking the interior with Zeila. They collected tributes from the Muslim emirates of Adal, Mora, Hobat and Jidaya.

Energizing trade and slavery expeditions, Islam penetrated farther south to be embraced by the rulers of the Sidama states of Hadya, Fatagar, Dawaro and Bali thereby ringing the massif of Christian Ethiopia.

The Muslim Sidama State of Hadya occupied the large territory between the Awash and Gibe rivers. Its Muslim ruling class prospered through commerce, and supplying eunuchs to the Arab lands where they fetched high prices. Its subjects were the Sidama-speaking people: the Gurage and the Chebo (a fusion of Gurage and Sidama).

The State of Fatagar was situated on the extreme southeastern buttresses of Shawa. Situated south of Shawa was the Muslim Sidama State of Dawaro (roughly present-day Arrsi). To the south of Dawaro was Bali stretching between the Wabi in the north and the Genale Doria in the south. The peace-loving Sidama of Bali lived by cultivating their fertile land. South of Bali was Borana, the home of the Oromo nomads.

## The Struggle Between Christian Ethiopia and Muslim Sultanates

In the last quarter of the thirteenth century, the center of Ethiopia moved from Lasta (the Zagwe Dynasty) to Tagulat (the Solomon Dynasty) in Amhara, from where the Ethiopian rulers, for many years to come, were engaged in life and death struggles with the Ifat Sultanate over the fertile regions of Shawa.

The Amhara rulers contained Islamic pressure, and extended their power over the Muslim sultanates in the early fourteenth century under Amde-Tseyon (1313-44). Thus, Ifat, Hadya, Fatagar, Dawaro and Bali were reduced to tributory "states." At the same time, the Shawa regions of Manz (Manzeh) and Zega were entirely annexed. Islamic influence quickly declined among the Sidama.

The Amhara rulers established territorial unity and strengthened the gult (fief) system to maintain themselves and their followers. Civil and religious institutions were rigorously codified, and literature and art began to flourish again.

Zara-Yacob (1434-68) from his center at Dabra-Berhan, overpowered the Muslim sultantates and cleansed Ifat of the Walasma elements who subsequently settled in Adal (comprising the regions of Afar, Danakil and Somali) with their new center at Dakar, a little southeast of the present-day Harar within the reach of the important trade routes to the port of Zeila.

During the reign of Zara-Yacob, urban establishments began to appear scattered south of Shawa, at Entoto, in the neighborhood of Mount Managasha, at Yarar, on the northern shores of Lake Zwai, and on the slopes of Jibat.

## The Invasion of Imam Ahmad and Ethiopia's Revival

Another big break in the development of Ethiopia occurred in the first half of the sixteenth century because of the great conquest of Imam Ahmed ibn Ibrahim AlGhazi of the Harar Emirate (an offshoot of the Adal Sultanate), assisted by the Ottoman Turks. Imam Ahmad (nicknamed Ahmad "Gragn"—the left-handed, by the Ethiopians) brought three-fourths of Ethiopia under his control for fifteen years.

His conquest was characterized by spoliations, burnings and massacre. Ethiopia underwent a terrible disaster. Its accumulated wealth was looted; its political organization, towns, ancient buildings, temples and many other invaluable objects were destroyed; and the orderly government and the arts of peace received an enormous setback. The people were forcibly Islamized en masse, peasants were pillaged and many fields went out of cultivation. As a consequence, a severe famine broke out in 1540 and 1543. Many Ethiopians were taken captives and sold into slavery. Ahmad and his followers acquired their wealth from trade in gold, ivory, civet, incense, myrrh, drugs and slaves.

Ethiopia revived in 1542 after Imam Ahmad was defeated and killed by the Semien army and the Portuguese, led by Gelawdewos (1540-1559), who readily reconquered most of the Empire. The Portuguese allied with Ethiopia to penetrate the Turkish blockade of the Red Sea trade, but soon turned hostile to the independent development of Ethiopia.

## The Oromo Expansion

In the second half of the sixteenth century, the Oromos ("Illm Orma"—sons of Oroma, their eponymous ancestor) began to migrate en masse to find new ranges from two main directions: one from the southwest along the corridor between Mount Walabu and Lake Abaya, and another from south ascending the Juba and Wabi river valleys.

Inspired by the cycle of Gadas (age-grade system), the Oromos raided and overran vast areas of land. By the early nineteenth century the Oromos had absorbed the Sidama of the south and southwest and formed the prosperous "states" of Jimma, Gera, Gomma, Limmu-Enarea, Nakamte Wallaga and Gudru.

The Oromo landed chiefs, the Abba Lafas, of the southwest acquired their wealth by taking over the Sidama states (the prosperous states of Enarea and Kaficho, whose kingdom extended from the fringe of the Sudanese lowlands in the west to the chain of lakes in the rift valley in the east, and from the northern bend of the Omo river in the north to Lake Rudolf in the south) and by developing commerce working in good terms with Muslim merchants from the Sudan and southeastern Ethiopia.

The Oromo rulers of the southwest embraced Islam, and their subjects followed suit. Trade in coffee, hides, skins, ivory and slaves became the main source of wealth and power for Aba Jifar of Jimma, surrounded by a league of Muslim trading centers.

In the west, Oromo chiefs arose in Gudru, Nakamte, Lagamara, Leka Kellem, Leka Sayo, and Nonno by acquiring wealth and influence through trade, collecting booty and owning land and slaves. Gama-Moras formed his Gudru state by accumulating wealth through trade in the Asandabo market where he collected tolls assisted by his own troops.

Unlike the Oromos of the south and southwest, the highland Oromos (Wallo, Yaju and Raya) came in close contact with the highland Amhara. They adopted settled agricultural life and the social and political institutions of the highland Amhara but maintained their Oromo identity by embracing Islam.

In the second half of the eighteenth century, the highland Oromos produced a nobility that was capable of penetrating the Court at Gondar. The Wallo Oromo chiefs, who were related to the sovereign, became provincial governors and a large number of Oromos were recruited into the imperial guards.

By the late eighteenth century, Ali, a ruling chief of the Yaju Oromos (Warra Shaikh), controlled the puppet emperor at Gondar and began to generate a hereditary Oromo dynasty in Bagemder.

The dominance of the Oromo nobility ignited internecine struggles thereby breaking up Ethiopia into a series of independent states: Bagemder, Gojjam, Damot, Tigrai, Lasta, the Eastern Oromo province and Shawa.

Each state conducted a separate development with its own army as a sovereign power engaging in treaty making with the West. The Church was the only common bond among the states. Shawa, largely cut off from the rest of the country by the Wallo Oromos, was able to make a considerable progress by expanding its frontiers under a series of kings.

## The Prominence of Gondar and Ethiopian Unity

By the beginning of the seventeenth century, Ethiopia definitely lost the southern territories, south of Shawa, to the Oromos. Ethiopia's territories were cut back to the natural boundaries of the Abai (Blue Nile) and Awash river with Oromo groups occupying the regions east of the plateau. State revenue was greatly reduced, and Ethiopia's development continued within the nucleus regions.

The greatest achievement in the second half of the seventeenth century was the establishment of Gondar in the northwest as the center of Ethiopia. The commercial significance of Gondar was considerable. Gondar provided market for local and imported goods, and agriculture in the surrounding areas flourished. The importance of the Sennar trade route increased and adjacent trading centers such as Emfras (a famous market place for civet and slaves) on the east coast of Lake Tana rapidly developed.

Gondar provided an urban climate for growth of merchants and artisans living in segregated communities: Christian Ethiopians, Muslim Ethiopians (Jabarti) and Jewish Ethiopians (Falashas). Muslim Ethiopians were debarred from owning land and engaging in agriculture, but became proficient in commerce and crafts and drew the trade of the region into their hands. Their social ostracism brought them into close contact with all other subjects: the Falasha, Sidama, Oromo and Shanquilla. In their travels from market to market, their religion began to cause a slow social fermentation among these peoples.

Besides commerce, Gondar owed it prominence to some administrative reforms carried out by Yesus The Great (1682-1706). The 'civil code' (Feteha-Negast) was revised and the laws of the land rectified. The rapacity of customs collectors was checked by establishing uniform rates throughout the country. This reform contributed greatly to the growth of trade.

In the second half of the nineteenth century, Tewodros of Kwara (1855-1867) conquered the divided regions and began the development of a unified Ethiopia with his center at Makdala. He divided the sovereign regions into small units, appointed his own trusted governors, and used the surplus to build his own army and support his administration.

Tewodros found the Church lands as the main source of maintenance for his numerous soldiers and administration. "What shall I eat and give to my soldiers?" Tewodros told the clerics, "You have taken all the lands, calling them 'land of the cross'." He had a good reason to hate the clerics, particularly the debtaras, who he said "wore turbans on their heads and neither fought nor paid taxes, but lived in cities with prostitutes and other people's wives." Consequently the Church elites turned out to be his arch enemies acting as prime movers and instigators of rebellions against him.

Tewodros was unparalleled by his predecessors in his reforms. Plowden explained Tewodros's courage for reforms in the following manner: ". . . He wishes to discipline his army and has in part already succeeded; to abolish the feudal system; to have paid governors and judges; and to disarm the people. He is just hearing in person the poorest people; he has stopped the system of bribes; he has, by his own example and by giving dowries and rewards to those who marry, discouraged polygamy and concubinage; he has forbidden the slave trade, and has tranquilized the whole country." He declared that he would convert swords and lances into plowshares and reaping hooks, and cause the plow-ox to be sold dearer than the noblest war horse.

But most of Tewodros's reforms were either frustrated or not enforced. He used excessive measures to have his orders obeyed and to unite the country. He decided either to convert or destroy the Muslim Oromos (Wallo and Yaju), the Falasha, Agaw, Wayto, and expell all other Muslims. Apparently he drew opposition from the Muslim population and remnants of the regional nobilities.

Tewodros was occupied largely with military matters. He built roads for military purposes and was very much attracted by the military technology of the West. This enabled him to acquire his own cannon and mortars with the assistance of Protestant missionaries from Switzerland.

The international situation did capture Tewodros's attention. Intending to penetrate the Turkish blockade of the Red Sea, Tewodros attempted to court Britain, who he thought was a "natural" (Christian) ally against a Muslim power. However, Britain had already allied with the Turks against Russia; and Tewodros's measures to impose the alliance upon the British invited one of their notorious expeditions—Napier's Expedition of 1868 that became the cause for the end of Tewodros, and the elevation of Yohannes (from Tambien in Tigrai) to the imperial throne.

During the reign of Yohannes (1872-1889), the European scramble for African colonies was at its peak. The development of Ethiopia was distracted by direct military and commercial penetration of Turco-Egypt (under Mohammed Ali), the Mahdists from the Sudan, and the European colonial powers.

Describing the difficult moments facing Yohannes, Jones and Monroe make the following comments: "The travelers of his generation were no longer free lances like Bruce and Plowden, but bagmen with machines and Western devices made in Birmingham and Leipzing and Lille and Brussels, and with a supply of blank treaty forms in their luggage. Through the whole of his reign, he was almost ceaselessly distracted by the aspiration, military and commercial, of outside powers."

Despite external disturbances, Yohannes made some efforts to continue the development of Ethiopia. He snatched Ethiopia out of isolation temporarily by expanding the empire along the Red Sea coast. He acquired Keren and secured the use of Massawa as a port in 1884.

Besides being a devout Christian, Yohannes saw Christianization of his empire as an effective means of uniting his people against outside menance. Thus, he ordered Muslim Ethiopians to embrace Christianity, build churches in their localities and pay tithe to their parish priests. Muslim state officials were ordered to accept baptism or resign their offices. Priority to own land was given to Christians. Consequently, the Muslim population was further alienated. Some of the smart Muslims who accumulated wealth from trade, managed to buy land ('worki'—gold) in Adwa, Hamasen, and Akala-Guzay disguised as Christians, and became the ristagnatat, the risti-owning class in the north.

## Eritrea

Treating making and military intrusions paid off for the Italians when they created their colony of Eritrea in 1890. The Italian colonialists, nipping from the African Red Sea coast and dismembering parts of northern Ethiopia carved out Eritrea.

The Italians used Eritrea mainly as a military base for further colonial intrusion, and as an outlet for the export of unprocessed products to Italy such as hides and skins, salt, mother-of-pearl, beewax and cement. They militarized the territory and deliberately neglected both agriculture and industry.

By discouraging industry in Eritrea they supplied unprocessed products to manufacturers in Italy. In order to stimulate recruiting, they denied agricultural concessions to Italian colonists. As a consequence, they did not have to alienate native land except from the rebellious chiefs.

Italian agriculture in Eritrea remained in its stifled infancy apart from such areas as Pendici on the eastern slopes of the altipiano and Tessenie and a few experimental farms. Some of the best agricultural land around Agordat and Tessenie was left unfarmed.

Italian colonists (numbering about 5,000 by 1935) worked mainly in garages or engineering shops or in minor businesses that catered for army needs. Trades and crafts that offered employment to Italians were closed to Eritreans. The occupations open to most Eritreans outside their community were those of office messenger, porter, stevedore, house or outdoor servant, odd-job, and soldiering in the colonial forces.

Inside the native community, things did not change much. The Bet-Asgada (the land-owning class) lived off the Tigre (the serf caste). Risti system (ancestoral land system) was converted into desa or shahina (village land), but the land-owning class still maintained its privileges and status.

In 1935, the campaign against Ethiopia led to a massive immigration of Italians to Eritrea. The campaign requirements and the consumption needs of the Italian colonists increased economic activities at the main centers. But agriculture and industry were energized by 1941 under the British Military Administration as a result of the Allied military needs and various American projects. Italians and Eritreans opened new businesses and nondurable consumer good industries. The number of native industrial workers increased. In addition to performing the simple manual tasks, more and more Eritreans worked as mechanics, machine-minders and machine-operators, bricklayers, masons, fitters, clerks, teachers, and medical technicians.

These new social groups produced by the colonial system provided the future political activists.

Upon liberation in 1941, and since the federation with Ethiopia, many Eritreans had come to Ethiopia to fill in positions in various technical and professional areas or to start private businesses.

# Imperial Expansion and Modernization

Ethiopia saw unprecedented political reunification, territorial expansion and modernization attempts in the late nineteenth and early twentieth centuries during the reign of Menelik (1889-1913). His famous reign—first as king of Shawa and then as Emperor of Ethiopia—coincided with the European Scramble for Africa and the first phase of the colonial period.

By opening the country to the west, Menelik enhanced his prosperity and influence and brought some of the advances of the modern world to Ethiopia for the first time. The external stimulus to development increased as many private entrepreneurs and self-employed concessioners came to Ethiopia.

The principal change in agriculture was the introduction of commercial farming for the first time into the country by foreign concessioners. Commercial cultivation of coffee began in the early twentieth century stimulated by the rapid increase in exports to the Sudan as a result of the opening of the inland port of Gambela on the Baro river. Foreign-owned coffee plantations emerged in Harar. The construction of the Addis Ababa-Jibouti railway facilitated the rapid growth of plantations. Some cotton, rubber and fiber plantations were initiated by foreign concessioners. Several modern cattle farms began enabling the country to export live meat by rail to Jibouti.

Commerce expanded as the opening of the Anglo-Ethiopian relations in 1897 led to the influx of Indian merchants. Other nationalities: Arabs, Armenians, French, Greeks and Jews played a prominent role in the development of import-export trade. Ethiopia's principal exports comprised ivory, gold, coffee, salt, civet, wax, hides and skins, oilseeds, grains, live animals, and coffee in exchange for textiles, cotton goods, firearms and some consumer goods such as sugar, soap and petroleum products.

Ethiopia witnessed the emergence of modern cities, typically urban in character, comprising a considerable number of merchants and artisans. The most important modern city, established by the Emperor himself in 1880's, was Addis Ababa (New Flower). The city of Addis Ababa played a significant role in the emergence of a market economy. Menelik carried out the main distribution of land for the city, and instituted private ownership of land in the surrounding rural areas that provided food and other supplies.

Addis Ababa became the center of innovation: modern houses, shops, flour mills, brick and liquor factories, oil presses and bakeries.

Menelik's palace was the nucleus of the emerging city of Addis Ababa. Governmental, diplomatic, agricultural and industrial affairs were concentrated at the palace. The requirements of the Emperor and his large entourage provided the market for the expansion of commercial enterprises in and around the compound. The palace enterprises employed some eight thousand people.

Another important city that came into existence in the early twentieth century was the railway center of Dire Dawa. The city of Dire Dawa grew rapidly due to its convenient location at the Addis Ababa-Jibouti railway that enabled it to steal the caravan routes of the south from the famous, old trading center of Harar.

The development of commerce was encouraged by the introduction of modern financial institutions and by the issuance of currency. Thus, a banking monopoly was granted by the Emperor's concession to the National Bank of Egypt—behind which stood an European banking group. The economy was enhanced by the introduction of such new advances as postal, telephone, telegram and electric light services. Printing presses and newspapers were introduced for the first time.

The foundation for modern education was laid in 1908 when the first public school came into existence to teach French, English, Italian and Amharic languages, mathematics, science and physical training. Various missionary societies became instrumental in introducing modern education to Ethiopia. Modern medicine was encouraged, and the Russian Red Cross that came to Ethiopia as a result of the famous Battle of Adwa (1896) provided help in spreading modern medical services in the country.

The empire and the resource base of Ethiopia was greatly extended and essential trade routes acquired by incorporating the Sidama-Oromo lands by military conquest. In most of these regions, the gult (fief) system was introduced or stimulated to maintain the imperial rulers, officials and followers (soldiers and clerics). Menelik's naftagnas (riflemen) introduced the plow, bureaucracy, literature and Christianity into the conquered lands.

Menelik enhanced his prosperity by collecting tributes from the conquered and dependent territories, selling concessions to foreigners, controlling trades of salt, ivory and gold, levying heavy percentages on the revenues of all foreigners and foreign companies, imposing dues on merchandise passing down the Addis Ababa-Jibouti railway, and doing lucrative business as chief money-lender to foreign concessioners. Menelik put very little of his fortune to commercial and technical use. Practically the whole of his money was spent on building his own army. Life in many parts of the country remained the same as it was in the previous centuries.

Haile Selassie (from 1928-35) advanced the modernization attempts started by Menelik. He sold the salt monopoly to a French company and some road and mining concessions that paid him modest royalties. He looked for foreign capital in 1930 to build a barrage at the Abai (Blue Nile) river. But, his attempt to acquire foreign capital was frustrated by the world economic crisis.

There were no significant economic changes during this period. A fundamental change occurred only in the creation of a loyal state.

Ethiopia was landlocked and had to face huge transportation costs. The Franco-Ethiopian Railway (a French monopoly) carried 70 percent of the exports while the remaining 20 percent was carried through Gambela and up to ten percent through the Italian colony of Eritrea. These routes were difficult, expensive and entailed long hauls through European colonies to reach the sea.

## Italian Colonialism

In 1936, the Italians occupied Ethiopia and began to create a colonial empire of Italian East Africa (consisting of Ethiopia, Eritrea, and Italian Somaliland).

The Italian colonialism was short-lived (1936-41) but brought dramatic impacts in such areas as infrastructure facilities and external trade. The Italians allocated £133 million for the first phase of colonial development, an amount by far larger than what the British allocated for their African colonies.

The Italians built, in record time, a network of roads and bridges bearing the marks of their engineering at its best. The huge investment in road works rapidly paid off as transportation costs of a ton per mile fell by more than sixty percent.

The Italian impact on Ethiopia's external trade was significant. Almost all the requirements for the development of Ethiopia and the consumption needs of large numbers of Italian colonists were to be imported from Italy; and Ethiopia's exports from now on had to go to Italy to finance the imports.

Ethiopia's imports increased astronomically while its exports fell since most of Ethiopia's 'traditional' export items (besides those needed by Italy) were not being exported now. The former foreign merchants who had experience in Ethiopia's import-export trade were expelled and replaced by Italian merchants.

The impact on agriculture was not as significant. Native land was alienated for white colonization. The main purpose was to cultivate cotton, vegetable fibers and oilseeds, and ranching.

Demobilized Italian soldiers were settled at Holetta and Bishoftu on 30,000 acres of land. Italian share tenants or small metayers coming from Romagna and Apulia were settled in Wagara (in Wallo province) and in Wachio (in Harar province). Another 55,000 acres was given to Italian yeoman-farmers along the roads from Addis Ababa to Dire Dawa and to Jimma. These farmers conducted experimental farms in new varities of cereals, vegetables, oil and cotton plants, fruit trees, and farmland animals: chickens, geese, turkeys and pigs. As a result of white colonization and pubic works (road construction, government buildings, etc.), there was a widespread wage-labor demand and conscription in the country-side.

As far as native agriculture is concerned, the Italians initiated what they called cotton districts where peasants were required to grow and sell cotton to the so-called development companies. On top of the cotton, the peasants were required to grow their own food crops. The Italians initiated agricultural settlement schemes for freed slaves. It was reported that some 165 schemes (villages of liberty, as the Italians called them), consisting of 125,000 freed slaves, were established. These schemes proved arduous at the beginning but showed encouraging results.

Prompted by the sudden colonial needs, the industrial progress under the Italians focused on the expansion of food-stuff processing factories (macaroni, biscuits, etc.), soap, matches and cigarette factories, breweries and distilleries, tanneries and footwear factories, textile factories and building material factories (cement, bricks, and tile). The Italians, in cooperation with German companies, conducted extensive surveys of the mineral wealth of Ethiopia for future commercial exploitation. No new mining techniques were introduced; the Italian companies still used indigenous methods and labor.

The Italians introduced some reforms and they were the major beneficiaries of these reforms. They introduced a number of new taxes in addition to carrying on with the Ethiopian tithe. There was a tax of one-thirtieth on the value of each head of livestock; a house tax and income tax, with further taxes on servants and improvements; taxes on the consumption of electricity, and even taxes on taxes for the purpose of bearing the expenses of collection.

The Italians boasted to reform the gult system. But except confiscating the property of the Emperor, the imperial family and rebellious nobles, they actually did nothing.

They issued a decree to liberate all slaves in Ethiopia, and this had a significant impact on the traditional system of slave and corvée labor. Former slaves settled on agricultural schemes, or were left with their old masters under metayer contracts, returned to their homes, or went into trade.

In order to undermine the power of the Church, the Italians took away the right of the Church to crown emperors; cut its Alexandrian connection thereby creating a puppet abuna; guaranteed respect for all possessions of the Church in return for preaching submission to the colonial government; and finally encouraged the spread of Islam.

## Modern Bureaucracy and Fall of A Dynasty

Liberation came to Ethiopia in 1941 when the Second World War was at its height. As a result of the 1942 treaty with Britain, Ethiopia began to receive British subsidies and advisers. A loan of £2.5 million, something new in the history of Ethiopia, was made available during 1942 and 1943 in return for free use of immovable property of Ethiopia required by the British forces during the War.

The demand created by the War revived Ethiopia's external trade. Most of the foreign merchants who were expelled by the Italians came back to take their key positions in trade and commerce.

One of the major reforms during the War period was the centralization of the tax system, for the first time, under ministry of finance. Thus, in 1941 land tax was collected in cash; and in 1944 a cash tax in lieu of tithe (asrat) was

introduced. The tax base of the state was expanded by introducing business profit taxes and personal income taxes.
Furthermore, the customs duty was reorganized.

Upon liberation, modern military and police forces were
established, soldiers were paid regular salaries, and provided
with food rations and uniforms. They lived in barracks but
without being detached from the public life. The armed forces
were modernized rapidly to become the most sophisticated
and strongest state apparatus.

By 1945 Ethiopia shifted its alliance to the United States of
America. A new currency was issued in 1945 with the help of
a large amount of silver loans received from the United
States under lend-lease agreement. Ethiopia joined the International Monetary Fund, and its contact with the West
reached unprecedented level during the post-War period.

The opportunities for external trade increased rapidly in
the post-War period. The principal exports of Ethiopia were
coffee, livestock and livestock products (live animals, fresh
and frozen meat, meat preparations and hides and skins),
oilseeds, and pulses: lentils, haricot beans and chickpeas.
Some progress was also made in the export of fish meal in the
1960's. Imports comprised various consumer goods (including
foodstuffs in times of famine) capital goods and development
project goods.

Ethiopia's export trade was mainly made up of coffee and
the country's foreign exchange earning capacity depended
on a single crop. About sixty percent of the total export value
was earned from coffee. The bulk of the coffee export went to
the United States of America. Ethiopia depended on a single
crop and single market for its foreign exchange earning.

Industrial activities have increased since the 1950's. The
state had a monopoly over key industries; in some instances

in joint venture with foreign capital. Despite encouragement by the government, foreign investment was not significant in the post-War period. Foreign loans were used to finance development projects.

The post-War industrial development focused on the expansion of food processing, beverage, textile, footwear and construction material factories. Ethiopia was able to reduce its import needs although all the consumer goods were not yet produced at home.

The increase in modern industries was accompanied by a growing number of factory workers. There were over 70,000 workers, organized into some 120 registered unions; the majority of the workers were unskilled, and the average wage for a worker was about $30 per month. The monthly wage, let alone to provide the basic necessities of a decent life for the worker and his family, was not even enough to buy the minimum basic food requirements. One of the reasons for abysmal low wages in Ethiopia was the absence of a minimum wage legislation.

Artisan operations, comprising weaving and tailoring of domestic clothes, ironwork, woodwork, pottery, shoe making, etc., were means of livelihood for many people in Ethiopia. But due to the competition from imported and locally manufactured goods, and lack of better equipment, funds, technical and managerial abilities, and incentives, some of the artisan activities declined while others disappeared completely.

In agriculture, there were some appearances of change during the post-War period. In 1966, the gult system was abolished; but former gultagnas were either made government officials or granted land; and became the landed-elites.

Former gultagnas and new landowners lived off the peasantry by renting out segments of their lands. Land grab-

bing by the powerful and the absence of contracts led to pro-
liferation of tenancy arrangements that were onerous in most
cases.

In 1967, an agricultural income tax on all agricultural
activities (excluding forestry, processing and cattle breeding)
was introduced, and the tax in lieu of tithe was abolished. The
object was to increase government revenue by taxing the
cultivator on income derived from cultivation, and the non-
cultivating landowner on income derived from renting his/
her land. The legislation drew opposition from the powerful
including the Church, and was not yet fully implemented in
the country by the early 1970's.

In the 1960's commercial farms began to penetrate some
areas in the countryside such as the Awash river valley and
the rift valley lakes as a result of concessions sold to foreigners and few local entrepreneurs. Most of these were efficient farms growing sugar cane, cotton, fruits and vegtables
for local consumption, enterprises and for exports. Commercial farming was still in its infancy in the 1970's, and over 90
percent of the agricultural production was under subsistence
crop and livestock farming. Thus, the majority of the people
were dirt poor scratching a living from the land or petty
trade.

The opportunities of the post-war period went largely to the
sovereign, imperial family, nobles and high officials in
Ethiopia. Firstly, upon liberation the imperial rulers and
their associates simply entered into the amenities and con-
veniences, which the Italian colonialists prepared for themselves. Henceforth, the imperial elites built their fortune as
the leading landowners and prominent officials in the newly
consituted government, assisted by a new class of civil servants.

Some of the old nobles were later replaced by their children and grandchildren who acquired modern education. The young nobles were accompanied by some of the modern intelligentsia who easily found niches for themselves in the various bureaucracies. As the young nobles took over, the aged found a place of honorable retirement in the crown council and the senate from where they opposed, assisted by their followers in the house of representatives, moderninzing reforms that threatened their interests.

Ethiopia's new modernizers came out of the armed forces. They assumed power in an atmosphere of growing unrest over high prices, the government's callous and incompetent handling of the tragic famine of 1973-74, as well as issues of corruption and maladministration. Assisted by progressive elements of the bureaucracy, they came forward with a socialist program for the development of Ethiopia. To make their revolution a success, they allied with the Soviet Union.

# I Introduction

1. Refer to Harvey Leibenstein, <u>Economic Backwardness and Economic Growth</u>, New York: John and Wiley, 1957; and Ragnar Nurkse, <u>Problems of Capital Formation in Underdeveloped Countries and Patterns of Trade and Development</u>, New York: Oxford University Press, 1967.
2. W.W. Rostow, <u>The Stages of Economic Growth: A Non-Communist Manifesto</u>, Cambridge: Cambridge University Press, 1960, p. 6.
3. Everett E Hagen, <u>The Economics of Development</u>, Homewood, Ill.: Richard D. Irwin, Inc., 1980, pp. 79-80.
4. Discussed in Henry Bienen, <u>Tanzania Party Transformation and Economic Development</u>, New Jersey: Princeton University Press, 1970, pp. 8-9.
5. Refer to Norman S. Buchanan and Howard S. Ellis, <u>Approaches to Economic Development</u>, New York: The twentieth Century Fund, 1955.
6. Discussed in Bienen, Op. Cit., p. 9.
7. Refer to Louis Snyder, <u>Varieties of Nationalism: A Comparative Study</u>, Hindsdale, Ill.: The Dryden Press, 1976, pp. 170-179.
8. See <u>National Unity and Regionalism in Eight African States</u>, ed. G.M. Carter, Ithaca: Cornell University Press, 1966, pp. 542-543.
9. Ibid., p. 163.
10. Much of the foundation for the modern day neo-Marxist Leninist theory was laid by Paul Baran, <u>The Political Economy of Growth</u>, New York: Monthly Review Press, 1968. Baran's basic thesis received considerable elaboration from Paul Sweezy, Andre Gunder Frank, Samir Amin, and etc.

11. Ibid., Giovanni Arrighi and John Saul, Socialism and Economic Development in Tropical Africa in Essays in The Political Economy of Africa, ed. Arrighi and Saul, New York: Monthly Review Press, 1973, pp. 11-43; and A.M. Babu, African Socialism or Socialist Africa? London: Zed Press, 1981.

12. Refer to Robert Brener, The Origins of Capitalist Development: A Critique of Neo-Smithian Marxism, in New Left Review, No. 104, July-August, 1977.

13. Robert C. Tucker, The Marxian Revolutionary Idea, New York: W.W. Norton & Co., Inc., pp. 92-93; 95-97; and 102-107.

14. Paul M. Sweezy, The Theory of Capitalist Development, New York: Monthly Reveiw Press, 1970. p. 308.

15. Ibid., pp. 326-327.

16. Ibid., pp. 327-328.

## II Theory and Reality

1. Ragnar Nurkse, Op. Cit., p. 4.

2. Ibid., pp. 4-5.

3. Ibid., p. 5.

4. Assefa Bequele and Eshetu Chole, A Profile of the Ethiopian Economy, Addis Ababa: Oxford University Press, 1969. p. 58.

5. See details in Richard Pankhurst, An Introduction to the Economic History of Ethiopia, London: Staples Printers Ltd., 1966, pp.307-308; and Mordechai Abir, Ethiopia: The Era of the Princes, New York: Praeger Publishers, 1968, pp. 42-72.

6. National Bank of Ethiopia, Annual Report, 1964-1973/ 74; and Commercial Bank of Ethiopia, Import Substitu-

tion in Ethiopia - Some Reflections, in <u>Market Report</u>, Sept. - Oct., 1974, pp. 5-6.

7. Everett E. Hagen, Op. Cit., pp. 85-86.

8. Ibid., p. 87.

9. Richard Pankhurst, <u>Economic History of Ethiopia, 1800-1935</u>, Addis Ababa: Haile Selassis I University Press, 1968, p. 723.

10. Margery Perham, <u>The Government of Ethiopia</u>, Evanston: Northwestern University Press, 1969, p. 177.

11. See Keith Griffin, <u>Underdevelopment in History</u>, in the <u>Political Economy of Development and Underdevelopment</u>, ed. Charles Wilber, 1979, pp. 84-86; and Roland Oliver and J.D. Fage, <u>A Short History of Africa</u>, Baltimore: Penguin Books Ltd., 1968, pp. 181-216.

12. In Robert L. Hess, <u>The Modernization of Autocracy</u>, Ithaca: Cornell University Press, 1970, p. 247.

13. See Everett E. Hagen, Op. Cit., pp. 39-90.

14. Donald Levine, <u>Wax and Gold: Tradition and Innovation in Ethiopian Culture</u>, Chicago: University of Chigago Press, 1965, pp. 275-276.

15. See Paul Baran, <u>The Political Economy of Growth</u>, New York: Monthly Review Press, 1968, p. 144.

16. Andre Gunder Frank, <u>The Development of Underdevelopment</u>, in <u>Imperialism and Underdevelopment,</u> ed., Robert I. Rhodes, New York: Monthly Review Press, 1970, p. 9.

17. Samir Amin, <u>Unequal Development: An Essay on the Social Formation of Peripheral Capitalism</u>, New York: Monthly Review Press, 1976, p. 333.

18. See Jones and Monroe, <u>A History of Ethiopia</u>, Oxford: Oxford University Press, 1935, pp. 134-135.

19. Margery Perham, Op. Cit., p. 181.

20. See Italian Library of Information, Development of Italian East Africa, New York City, 1940, pp. 37; 103-107; and Greenfield, Ethiopia: A New Political History, London: Pal Mall Press, 1965, p. 237

21. See Margery Perham, Op. Cit., pp. 181, 184; Italian Library of Information, Op. Cit., pp. 63, 40-55; and Greenfield, Op. Cit., p. 237.

22. Perham, Op. Cit., p. 185.

23. Jones and Monroe, Op. Cit., pp. 165-172; and Perham, Op. Cit., p. 180.

24. See Commercial Bank of Ethiopia, Share of Ethiopian Capital in New Business Formation During 1970, in Market Report, December, 1970, p. 2.

25. Everett E. Hagen, Op. Cit., p. 315.

26. See AFRICA NEWS, Oct. 12, 1979, and AFRICA BUSINESS, Oct., 1979, p. 17.

27. Refer to Joseph S. Nye, Jr., Multinational Corporations in World Politics, in FOREIGN AFFAIRS, Vol. 53, No. I, Oct. 1974, pp. 165-166; Mordechai Kreinin, International Economics: A Policy Approach, New York: Harcourt Brace Jovanovich, Inc., 1979, pp. 359-360; and Investment in China, in The Economist, April 2-8, 1983, pp. 77-78.

28. The experience of Brazil is discussed as an example by Arthur MacEwan, New Light on Dependency and Dependent Development, in Monthly Review, January, 1983, pp. 12-25.

29. See Willy Brant, North-South: A Program for Survival, Cambridge: The MIT Press, 1980, pp. 187-188; and Everett E. Hagen, Op. Cit., p. 318.

30. Details in Spencer Triningham, Islam in Ethiopia, London: Frank Cass & Co., 1965, p. 60; Jones and Monroe,

124

Op. Cit., pp. 45-46.

31. Addis Hiwet, <u>Ethiopia: From Autocracy to Revolution</u>, in REVIEW OF AFRICAN POLITICAL ECONOMY, London, 1975, and Bereket Habte Selassie, <u>Conflict and Intervention in the Horn of Africa</u>, New York: <u>Monthly Review Press</u>, 1980.

32. Details in Allan Hoben, <u>Land Tenure Among the Amhara of Ethiopia</u>, Chicago: University of Chicago Press, 1973, p. 3, and Donald Levine, Op. Cit., pp. 1-4.

33. Jean Doresse, <u>Ethiopia</u>, London: Elek Books Ltd., 1956, p. 115, and Mordechai Abir, Op. Cit., pp. xviii-xix.

34. See Hess, <u>Ethiopia</u>, ed. Carter, Op. Cit., pp. 443-466.

35. Details in Donald Levine, <u>Greater Ethiopia</u>, Chicago: The University of Chicago Press, 1973, p. 3, and Donald Levine, Op. Cit., pp. 1-4.

36. Geoffrey Wheeler, <u>Racial Problems in Soviet Muslim Asia</u>, London: Institute of Race Relations, Oxford University Press, 1967.

37. See Basil Dmystyshn, <u>USSR A Concise History</u>, New York: Charles Scribner's Sons, 1978, pp. 76-80.

38. Greenfield, Op. Cit., pp. 303-306; Hess, <u>Ethiopia</u>, ed.Carter, Op. Cit., pp. 503-504.

39. Peter Waterman, <u>Workers in the Third World</u>, in <u>Monthly Review</u>, Sept., 1977, pp. 50-64.

40. See Karl Polanyi, <u>The Great Transformation</u>, Boston: Beacon Press, 1957, pp. 152-153.

# III Problems of Development and Nation Building

1. For contributory factors to economic development, refer to Robert L. Heilbroner, <u>The Making of Economic Society,</u> Englewood Cliffs, N.J.: Prentice Hall, Inc., 1980, pp. 73-80.

2. See Allen Hoben, Op. Cit,. and John Bruce, Land Reform Planning and Indigenous Communal Tenures, S.J.D. Thesis in the School of Law of the University of Wisconsin-Madison, 1976.
3. See details in Comercial Bank of Ethopia, Agrarian Reform and Economic Development: The Ethiopian Case, in Market Report, Jan.-Feb., 1974.
4. In Donald Levine, Op. Cit., pp. 86-88.
5. Ibid., p. 88.
6. Allan Hoben, Op. Cit., pp. 226-229.
7. Details in Tesfai Tecle, Rural Development in Ethiopia Past, Present and Future, in African Rural Employment Research Network, Michigan State University, 1974, and Hailu Wolde Emanuel, Land Tenure, Land Use and Development in the Awash Valley, Land Tenure Center, University of Wisconsin-Madison, December, 1973.
8. John Bruce, Ethiopia: Nationalization of Rural Lands Proclamation, 1975, in Land Tenure Newsletter, No. 47, Jan.-March, 1975, and Ronald James Clark, The Ethiopian Land Reform - Scope, Accomplishments and Future Objectives, in FAO, Land Reform, Land Settlement and Cooperatives, No. 2, 1975.
9. The Campaign to Restructure Ethiopia's Economy, in AFRICA BUSINESS, Oct., 1979, pp. 16-17.
10. Information about the current situation is reported in National Geographic Society, May, 1983, pp. 614-644.
11. Spencer Trimingham, Op. Cit., pp. 44-48.
12. Mordechai Abir, Op. Cit., pp. 70-71.
13. Donald Levine, Op. Cit., p. 189.
14. Ibid., pp. 81-82.
15. Jones and Monroe, Op. Cit., pp. 120-121.
16. See Allan Hoben, Op. Cit., pp. 182-184.

17. In Donald Levine, Op. Cit., pp. 127-139; 191-194 and Greenfield, Op. Cit., pp. 311-319.

18. Return to the Source: Selected Speaches of Amilcar Cabral, ed. African Information Service, New York: Monthly Review Press, 1973, pp. 77-78.

19. See details in Meier and Baldwin, Economic Development: Theory, History, Policy, New York: John Wiley & Sons, Inc., pp. 245-254, and Evertt E. Hagen, Op. Cit., pp. 286-287.

20. Gary M. Walton and Ross M. Robertson, History of the American Economy, New York: Harcourt Brace Jovanovich, 1983, pp. 242-244; and Harry Magdoff, Capital, Technology, and Development, in Monthly Review, January, 1976, pp. 9-10.

21. Mordechai E. Kreinin, Op. Cit., p. 301.

22. See Paul Baran Op. Cit., pp. 158-160.

23. For further information about the Soviet System, refer to Gregory and Stuart, Comparative Economic Systems, Boston: Houghton Mifflin Co., 1980, pp. 200-238.

24. Alec Nove, An Economic History of the USSR, Baltimore: Pelican Books Ltd., 1975, pp. 11-28.

25. Franklin W. Houn, A Short History of Chinese Communism, Englewood Cliffs, N.J.: Prentice Hall, Inc., 1973, pp. 5-6.

26. John Gurley, China's Economy and the Maoist Strategy, New York: Monthly Reveiw Press, 1976.

27. Edgar Snow, Red China Today, New York: Random House, 1970, pp. 62-63, and Franklin W. Houn, Op. Cit., p. 4.

28. See Dwight H. Perkins, Agricultural Development in China, 1368-1968, Chicago: Aldine, 1968; and Ester Boserup, The Conditions of Agricultural Growth: The

Economics of Agrarian Change and Population Pressure, Adline, 1968.

29. Richard Pankhurst, Economic History of Ethiopia, Op. Cit., p. 10.

30. See Kofi R. H. Darkwah, Shawa, Menelik and the Ethiopian Empire, 1813-1889, London: Heinemann Educational Books Ltd., 1975, p. 148.

31. In Commercial Bank of Ethiopia, Import-Substitution in Ethiopia, Op. Cit., pp. 5-7.

32. Louis L. Snyder, Op. Cit., pp. 10-11; 73-75; 202-204.

33. See the New Left criticism against contemporary capitalism in Gregory and Stuart, Op. Cit., pp. 96-97.

34. Barrington Moore, Social Origins of Dictatorship and Democracy, Boston: Beacon Press, 1966, p. 414.

35. Ruth First, Power in Africa, New York: Patheon Books, 1970, p. 16.

36. Louis L. Snyder, Op. Cit., pp. 73-74.

37. Jack Woddis, Africa: The Way Ahead, New York: national Publishers, 1964, pp. 97-101. The architect of the one-party state in Africa is Julius Nyerere, Ujamaa: Essays on Socialism, Dar-es-Salaam: Oxford University Press, 1968, Michael Manley, Jamaica: Struggle in the Periphery, London: Third World Media Ltd., 1982, pp. 50-53.

38. Frantz Fanon, The Pitfalls of National Consciousness in The Wretched of the Earth, New York: Grove Press, Inc., 1963, pp. 164-165; 168; 170 & 171.

39. Robert Heilbroner, Op. Cit., pp. 256-257.

40. See National Geographic Society, May, 1983.

## IV Prospects for Development and Nation Building

1. See Gregory and Stuart, Op. Cit., pp. 220-221.
2. In John Gurley, Op. Cit., pp. 241-250.
3. For further information about the contract system, refer to William H. Hinton, "A Trip to Fengyang County: Investigating China's New Family Contract System," in Monthly Review, Nov., 1983, pp. 1-28.
4. Gregory and Stuart, Op. Cit., p. 219.
5. Refer to Peter Dorner, Transformation of U.S. Agriculture, The Past Forty Years, Land Tenure Center, University of Wisconsin-Madison, July 14-22, 1977.
6. Wylde, quoted in Donald Levine, Op. Cit., p. 4.
7. Commercial Bank of Ethiopia, Cooperatives - Whose Servants? in Market Report, Sept.-Oct., 1973, p. 3.
8. Ibid., pp. 8-9.
9. For details, see John Cohen, Rural Change in Ethiopia: The Chilalo Agricultural Development Unit, in Economic Development and Cultural Change, July, 1974, pp. 593-608.
10. Commercial Bank of Ethiopia, The "Package Program" Approach for Ethiopian Development, in Market Report, March, 1971.
11. Tesfai Tecle, Op. Cit., p. 20.
12. Public Ownership of Rural Lands Proclamation, No. 31 of 1975, in Negarit Gazeta, 34th year, No. 26, April, 1975.
13. See Alan Hoben, Amhara Land Tenure, The Dynamics of Cognative descent in Ethiopia, Addison Maine, Sept., 1971, Land Tenure Center, University of Wisconsin-Madison, mimeo. p. 153; and John Bruce, Op. Cit., pp. 6-11.

14. Michael Stahl, New Seeds in Old Soil, A Study of the Land Reform Process in Western Wallaga, Ethiopia. 1975-1976, Research Report No. 40, Uppsala: The Scandinavian Institute of African Studies, 1977, pp.25-26, p. 41.

15. Ibid., p. 30, and Alula Abate and Tesfaye Teklu, Land Reform and Peasant Association in Ethiopia - Case Studies of Two Widely Differing Regions, in Northeast African Studies, Fall, 1980, p. 23.

16. Details in Fekadu Wakjira, Recent Institutional Innovations and Structural Transformation of Rural Economies in Ethiopia, Land Tenure Center, University of Wisconsin-Madison, July, 1977.

17. Commercial Bank of Ethiopia, Agrarian Reform and Economic Development, Op. Cit., p. 27.

18. See Gail Simpson, Socio-Political Aspects of Settlement Schemes in Ethiopia, in Land Reform, Land Settlement and Cooperatives, No. 2, 1976, p. 36, and Fakadu Wakjira, Op. Cit., pp. 8 and 8A.

19. See Special Study, Agriculture in Africa, in AFRICA, July, 1977 and Sept. 1977.

20. William Alan, The African Husbandman, New York: Barns and Noble, 1965, and Riddell, Parsons and Kanel, Land Tenure Issues in African Development, Land Tenure Center, University of Wisconsin-Madison, June, 1978, pp. 24-26.

21. Ethiopia's average annual growth rate of agricultural production fell to 0.9% in 1970-82 from a 2.2% in 1960-70, and the average index of food production per capita in 1980-82 dropped to 82% of the 1967-71 level. IBRD/The World Bank, World Development Report 1984, New York: Oxford University Press, 1984, pp. 220 & 228.

22. The idea of composting and organic farming methods is suggested for Africa in AFRICA NEWS, April, 30, 1984, pp. 6-8 & 11; and May 7, pp. 1-4, & 11.
23. Further details in Richard B. Ford, "Environment: Putting the Problems in Context,"in Africa Report, May-June, 1978, "Deforestation: An Ecological Challenge," in AFRICA NEWS, Nov. 23, 1979, and "Combatting the Creepting Desert: A Special Study, Agriculture in Africa, in AFRICA, July, 1977.
24. Further details in Johan Holemberg, Op. Cit., pp. 24-26.
25. Jack Woddis, Op. Cit., p. 24.
26. The World Bank, Accelerated Development in Sub-Sahara Africa, An Agenda for Action, Washington D.C., IBRD/The World Bank, 1981, p. 5.
27. The rising military spending in Africa is draining funds which otherwise could be used for productive purposes such as agricultural development. For example, Africa's public expenditure per soldier in 1978 was $8,500 while public expenditure per capita was only $20. (For Ethiopia, it was $2,500 and $120 respectively.) In Africa Report, May-June, 1978.
28. For the first group, see The World Bank, Op. Cit., p. 4, and for the second group, refer to Cheryl Payer, in AFRICA NEWS, May 30, 1983, p. 4.
29. For problems with the IMF prescriptions, refer to Monthly Review, Jan., 1984, pp. 1-10.
30. Michael Manley, Op. Cit., p. 165.
31. The World Bank, Op. Cit., p. 7.
32. The Politics of Foreign Assistance, in AFRICA REPORT, May-June, 1980, p. 50.
33. Ibid., p. 51.
34. U.S Foreign Policy in the 1980's, in Monthly Review,

April, 1980, pp. 3-4, & 6.

35. See Andreas Papandreou, <u>Confrontation and Coexistence</u>, in <u>Monthly Review</u>, April, 1978, p. 16.

36. Ibid., pp. 16 & 20; and Michael Manely, Op. Cit., pp. 25-39; and 175-183.

37. Andreas Papandreou, Op. Cit., pp. 14-15.

38. For information about the 1960 Coup, see Greenfield, Op. Cit., pp. 375-418.

39. See <u>Africa News</u>, Oct. 8, 1984, pp. 14-15.

40. For the weaknesses of the one-party state today, refer to <u>The Economist</u>, Oct. 1, 1983, p. 10.

41. See Louis L. Snyder, Op. Cit., pp. 177-178.

42. <u>The Economist</u>, Nov., 3, 1983, p. 44; and <u>Africa News</u>, Nov. 19, 1984, p. 3.

43. <u>Africa News</u>, Nov. 19, 1984, p. 4.

Index